SPACs and Alternative Paths to Going Public

How Special Purpose Acquisition Companies Create Faster Public Listings

By Joe Correa

Published by Live Stronger Faster

This book is for educational and informational purposes only. The author and publisher are not engaged in rendering legal, financial, or other professional advice. Readers should consult a qualified professional before making any financial decisions.

First Edition

Table of Contents

Introduction 5

Chapter 1: Understanding SPACs and the Evolution of Alternative Public Offerings.......15

Chapter 2: How SPAC Transactions Work Step by Step.........33

Chapter 3: The Advantages and Risks of SPACs for Founders and Investors.......52

Chapter 4: Reverse Mergers and Other Alternative Paths to Public Markets.......72

Chapter 5: Direct Listings and the Future of Public Market Access.......91

Chapter 6: How Market Cycles and Investor Psychology Shape Alternative Public Offerings.......109

Chapter 7: Institutional Investors, PIPE Financing, and Capital Raising Strategy.......127

Chapter 8: Regulation, Governance, and the Responsibilities of Public Companies.......146

Chapter 9: Building Long-Term Wealth Through Public Companies and Equity Ownership.......165

Chapter 10: The Future of Public Markets, Innovation, and Global Wealth Creation.......183

Final IPO Thoughts.......201

Table of Contents

Introduction 5

Chapter 1: Understanding SPACs and the Evolution of Alternative Public Offerings....13

Chapter 2: How SPAC Transactions Work Step by Step......33

Chapter 3: The Advantages and Risks of SPACs for Founders and Investors......52

Chapter 4: Reverse Mergers and Other Alternative Paths to Public Markets......72

Chapter 5: Direct Listings and the Future of Public Market Access......91

Chapter 6: How Market Cycles and Investor Psychology Shape Alternative Public Offerings......109

Chapter 7: Institutional Investors, PIPE Financing, and Capital Raising Strategy......127

Chapter 8: Regulation, Governance, and the Responsibilities of Public Companies......146

Chapter 9: Building Long-Term Wealth Through Public Companies and Equity Ownership......165

Chapter 10: The Future of Public Markets, Innovation, and Global Wealth Creation......183

Final IPO Thoughts......201

Introduction

The journey to taking a company public has evolved dramatically over the past several decades. While traditional initial public offerings, commonly known as IPOs, have long been considered the gold standard for entering the public markets, they are no longer the only path available for companies seeking public capital, liquidity, expansion opportunities, and long-term wealth creation. In recent years, Special Purpose Acquisition Companies, often referred to as SPACs, along with reverse mergers and other alternative listing methods, have transformed the landscape of public offerings. These alternatives have opened doors for entrepreneurs, investors, startups, growth-stage companies, and even established private businesses that previously may not have qualified for or desired a traditional IPO process.

This book is designed to help you understand one of the most discussed and misunderstood topics in modern capital markets: SPACs and alternative public listing strategies. Whether you are an entrepreneur, investor, startup founder, financial professional, or simply someone interested in how companies rapidly achieve billion-dollar public valuations, this book will provide a foundational and practical understanding of how these transactions work, why they exist, and how they can create extraordinary opportunities for wealth creation.

For many years, taking a company public was viewed as a long, expensive, highly regulated process that only the largest and most sophisticated businesses could realistically achieve. Companies often spent years preparing audited financial statements, meeting strict exchange requirements, hiring major investment banks, conducting roadshows, and negotiating underwriting agreements before finally ringing the opening bell on a stock exchange. While traditional IPOs remain extremely important, they are not always the best fit for every business. Some companies need faster access to capital. Others want more pricing certainty. Some seek strategic partnerships or wish to avoid the unpredictability of traditional IPO market conditions. This is where SPACs and alternative listing structures enter the picture.

A SPAC, or Special Purpose Acquisition Company, is essentially a publicly traded shell company created for the purpose of acquiring or merging with a private company. Unlike a traditional operating company, a SPAC initially has no products, services, or active business operations. Instead, it raises money from investors through its own IPO and then seeks to identify a promising private company to merge with. Once the merger occurs, the private company effectively becomes publicly traded without going through the traditional

IPO route. This process has become known as the "backdoor IPO" or "fast-track IPO" process because it can significantly accelerate a company's journey to the public markets.

The rise of SPACs created enormous excitement throughout the financial world because they offered flexibility, speed, and access to growth capital at unprecedented levels. During periods of market enthusiasm, hundreds of SPACs were formed by experienced executives, private equity firms, celebrities, hedge fund managers, venture capitalists, and industry specialists. Billions of dollars flowed into these vehicles as investors searched for the next high-growth opportunity. Companies in industries such as electric vehicles, artificial intelligence, biotechnology, renewable energy, fintech, space technology, and digital platforms increasingly explored SPAC mergers as alternatives to traditional IPOs.

However, alongside the opportunities came substantial risks and challenges. Many companies entering the public markets through SPACs struggled with unrealistic valuations, weak operational performance, regulatory scrutiny, and investor disappointment. Some SPAC transactions generated extraordinary wealth for founders and early investors, while others became cautionary tales about hype, speculation, and poor financial discipline. Understanding both the advantages and the dangers of SPACs is essential for anyone considering this path or investing in companies that pursue it.

One of the most important concepts you will learn throughout this book is that public markets are not simply about raising money. Public markets are fundamentally about liquidity, valuation, visibility, scalability, and wealth creation. A successful public listing can transform a relatively unknown private business into a globally recognized enterprise. It can allow founders to access large pools of institutional capital, acquire other companies using stock, attract top executive talent with equity compensation, and create liquidity for early investors and employees. In many cases, going public becomes the catalyst for generational wealth creation.

This wealth creation process is often misunderstood by people outside the financial world. Many assume that founders become wealthy because they suddenly receive large salaries after taking their companies public. In reality, most founder wealth is created through ownership of equity. When a company's valuation increases from a few million dollars to hundreds of millions or even billions, the value of the founder's shares can increase exponentially. SPACs and alternative public listing methods can accelerate this process by providing quicker access to public market valuations and capital inflows. At the same time, alternative listing structures have democratized certain aspects of capital markets. In the past, access to high-growth private companies was often limited to venture capital firms, institutional investors, and ultra-wealthy individuals. Today, alternative public offerings can allow retail investors to participate earlier in the growth cycle of emerging businesses. While this creates opportunity, it also creates volatility and risk. Understanding how these deals are structured, financed, marketed, and executed becomes critically important for investors seeking to protect capital while participating in high-growth opportunities.

Throughout this book, you will also learn that SPACs are only one part of a broader ecosystem of alternative public offerings. Reverse mergers, direct listings, OTC market transitions, dual listings, and hybrid financing structures all play important roles in the modern financial landscape. Companies today have more strategic options than ever before when deciding how to access public capital markets. Each path carries unique advantages, disadvantages, costs, regulatory requirements, and long-term implications for shareholders and management teams.

One reason alternative public offerings have gained popularity is because the financial world itself has changed. Technology has accelerated communication, investing, and market participation. Social media, digital brokerages, online investing communities, and global access to information have fundamentally reshaped how companies build investor interest and raise capital. The rise of retail investing platforms introduced millions of new participants into the stock market. As a result, companies increasingly seek flexible public listing strategies that align with modern investor behavior and evolving capital market dynamics.

The global startup ecosystem has also expanded dramatically. Entrepreneurs around the world are building innovative businesses faster than ever before. Industries such as artificial intelligence, software-as-a-service, biotechnology, digital finance, renewable energy, robotics, and online education have experienced explosive growth. Many of these companies require substantial capital to scale operations, acquire customers, develop products, and compete internationally. Alternative public offering structures provide additional pathways to secure that growth capital.

As you progress through this book, you will discover that successful SPAC and reverse merger transactions require far more than hype or financial engineering. Long-term success still depends on business fundamentals, leadership quality, operational execution, financial controls, transparency, scalability, and investor confidence. Public markets can reward companies with extraordinary valuations, but they can also punish weak management, unrealistic projections, and poor governance practices. Companies entering the public markets must understand the immense responsibilities that come with being publicly traded.

You will also learn about the role of sponsors, PIPE investors, underwriters, institutional investors, regulatory agencies, auditors, attorneys, and investment bankers in the SPAC ecosystem. These players collectively shape the success or failure of a transaction. Understanding their incentives and responsibilities provides deeper insight into how deals are negotiated and why some transactions outperform others.

Another major theme of this book is timing. Market conditions play a powerful role in determining whether a SPAC or alternative public offering succeeds. Bull markets often create enthusiasm, high valuations, and easier capital raising environments. Bear markets, rising interest rates, economic uncertainty, or regulatory crackdowns can dramatically reduce investor appetite for speculative growth companies. Founders must understand how economic cycles impact capital markets and how strategic timing can influence valuation outcomes.

In addition to discussing the mechanics of SPACs and reverse mergers, this book will explore the psychology behind public market investing. Investor sentiment, media narratives, momentum trading, institutional confidence, and speculative behavior all influence stock performance. Public companies operate in an environment where perception can significantly impact valuation. Learning how public narratives are created and sustained becomes essential for founders and investors alike.

One of the greatest lessons in capital markets is that wealth creation is rarely accidental. The founders, executives, investors, and companies that achieve lasting success often possess a deep understanding of timing, capital structure, investor psychology, market positioning, and long-term strategic planning. Going public is not simply an endpoint; it is often the beginning of an entirely new phase of growth, responsibility, and opportunity.

This book is intended to provide a practical, realistic, and balanced understanding of SPACs and alternative public listing methods. It is not designed to promote speculation or unrealistic expectations. Instead, it aims to help readers develop financial literacy, strategic thinking, and a deeper appreciation for how modern capital markets function. Whether you eventually decide to launch a startup, invest in public companies, advise businesses, or simply expand your financial knowledge, understanding these concepts can significantly improve your perspective on wealth creation and entrepreneurship. The future of public markets will likely continue evolving as technology, regulation, globalization, and investor behavior change over time. New financing structures may emerge. Existing models may adapt. Some strategies will succeed while others disappear. But one reality will remain constant: companies that successfully combine innovation, scalability, leadership, and access to capital will continue creating extraordinary wealth opportunities.

As you begin this book, approach the subject with curiosity, discipline, and critical thinking. Some of the companies discussed throughout these pages may become major global enterprises. Others may fail completely. That is the nature of entrepreneurship and investing. The goal is not to eliminate risk entirely, but rather to understand how risk, capital, valuation, and opportunity interact within the financial markets.

SPACs and alternative public offerings represent one of the most fascinating developments in modern business finance because they sit at the intersection of entrepreneurship, investing, innovation, speculation, and wealth creation. Understanding how these structures work can provide valuable insight into the future of business growth and personal financial opportunity. In many ways, these alternative public listing methods symbolize the evolving nature of capitalism itself—faster, more global, more technology-driven, and increasingly accessible to a wider range of participants. The companies of tomorrow may not all follow the traditional path to becoming public enterprises. Some will emerge through SPAC mergers. Others through direct listings, reverse mergers, tokenized assets, or entirely new financial structures yet to be invented. By understanding these evolving pathways today, you place yourself in a stronger position to recognize future opportunities, evaluate risks intelligently, and potentially participate in the next generation of wealth creation through the public markets.

Chapter 1

Understanding SPACs and the Evolution of Alternative Public Offerings

For decades, the traditional initial public offering represented one of the most prestigious milestones a company could achieve. Going public through a traditional IPO symbolized that a private business had reached a level of financial maturity, operational stability, and investor appeal sufficient to enter the public capital markets. Companies that successfully completed IPOs often experienced dramatic increases in visibility, valuation, investor access, and long-term growth opportunities. However, as financial markets evolved and entrepreneurship accelerated worldwide, the limitations of the traditional IPO process became increasingly apparent. Many private companies found the process expensive, time-consuming, unpredictable, and highly dependent on market conditions. As a result, alternative methods for becoming publicly traded began attracting greater attention from entrepreneurs, investors, and financial professionals seeking more flexible solutions.

One of the most important developments in this evolution was the rise of the Special Purpose Acquisition Company, commonly known as a SPAC. Although SPACs existed for many years in smaller forms, they gained enormous popularity during periods of strong market growth when investors aggressively sought access to innovative, high-growth businesses. SPACs created a faster and often more flexible path for companies to access the public markets. In many ways, they transformed how people viewed the concept of going public itself.

To fully understand why SPACs became so influential, it is important to first understand the traditional IPO process and the challenges associated with it. In a conventional IPO, a private company hires investment banks to underwrite the offering. The company must prepare extensive financial statements, complete audits, comply with regulatory requirements, draft registration documents, conduct investor roadshows, and negotiate pricing with institutional investors. This process can take many months or even years depending on the size and complexity of the company. During this time, market conditions may change dramatically. A market downturn, geopolitical event, interest rate increase, or weak investor sentiment can negatively impact the valuation or timing of the IPO.

In addition, traditional IPO pricing itself can be uncertain. Many companies spend years building value only to face unexpected volatility during the final pricing process. In some cases, companies believe their shares were underpriced by underwriters, leaving substantial money on the table after the stock begins trading publicly. Other companies may experience disappointing demand or struggle to attract sufficient institutional interest. For growth-stage businesses operating in rapidly evolving industries, this uncertainty can create enormous strategic pressure.

SPACs emerged as an alternative that addressed several of these challenges. A SPAC is essentially a publicly traded shell company created solely to raise money and eventually merge with a private company. Unlike a traditional operating business, a SPAC initially has no commercial operations. Instead, its primary purpose is to identify a target company, negotiate a merger, and bring that company into the public markets. Investors who purchase shares in the SPAC are essentially betting on the expertise and reputation of the SPAC sponsors, who are responsible for identifying promising acquisition opportunities.

The structure of a SPAC transaction differs significantly from a traditional IPO. Instead of the private company directly selling shares to the public through an underwritten offering, the SPAC itself first raises money through its own IPO. Once capital is secured, the SPAC sponsors search for a private company to merge with. After negotiations are completed and shareholder approvals are obtained, the private company merges into the SPAC and becomes publicly traded. This process is commonly referred to as a "de-SPAC transaction."

One reason SPACs gained popularity is because they can offer greater certainty around valuation. In a traditional IPO, the final valuation is often determined near the pricing date and can fluctuate based on market demand. In a SPAC merger, however, the valuation is negotiated directly between the SPAC sponsors and the target company. This can provide founders and early investors with greater predictability regarding ownership percentages and potential proceeds.

Speed also became a major advantage. Many private companies viewed SPACs as a faster route to public markets compared to traditional IPOs. In industries driven by innovation and competition, speed can be extremely valuable. Companies developing cutting-edge technologies often need rapid access to capital in order to expand operations, hire talent, develop products, or acquire competitors. The ability to enter public markets more quickly can create a strategic advantage in fast-moving sectors.

Another important factor contributing to the growth of SPACs was investor appetite for emerging industries. During periods of market optimism, investors became highly interested in sectors such as electric vehicles, renewable energy, fintech, biotechnology, artificial intelligence, online platforms, and space technology. Many SPACs specifically targeted these industries because traditional IPO investors sometimes hesitated to support companies with limited operating histories or uncertain profitability. SPACs allowed these growth-oriented companies to tell a forward-looking story centered on future potential rather than solely historical performance.

This ability to present forward projections became another distinguishing feature of SPAC transactions. In traditional IPOs, companies face strict limitations regarding future financial projections due to regulatory concerns. SPAC mergers, however, historically allowed greater flexibility in presenting long-term growth forecasts to investors. This enabled companies to market ambitious visions for future expansion, market dominance, and technological disruption. While this flexibility created excitement, it also introduced substantial risks when projections proved unrealistic or overly optimistic.

As SPAC popularity increased, a wide range of influential individuals entered the market as sponsors. Hedge fund managers, private equity firms, venture capitalists, former executives, athletes, entertainers, and even celebrities launched SPACs. The reputation of the sponsors often played a major role in attracting investors. Investors believed that experienced sponsors possessed the industry expertise, relationships, and strategic insight necessary to identify high-potential acquisition targets.

However, despite the enthusiasm surrounding SPACs, the structure itself carries important complexities and risks. One major issue involves dilution. SPAC sponsors typically receive founder shares, often referred to as the "promote," which can represent a substantial ownership stake in the post-merger company. Additional dilution may occur through warrants, PIPE financing, and redemption rights. As a result, the ownership percentages of existing shareholders may decrease significantly after the transaction closes.

Another important risk involves investor redemptions. SPAC investors generally have the right to redeem their shares for cash before the merger is completed if they do not approve of the proposed transaction. High redemption rates can reduce the amount of capital available to the merged company and may create financial instability. Companies entering SPAC mergers must carefully manage investor communication and market perception in order to maintain confidence throughout the transaction process.

Regulatory scrutiny also increased as the SPAC market expanded. Financial regulators became concerned about accounting practices, disclosure quality, aggressive projections, conflicts of interest, and speculative investor behavior. Some companies that entered public markets through SPACs experienced sharp stock price declines after failing to meet expectations. These failures highlighted the importance of operational discipline, realistic financial planning, and transparent communication with investors.

Despite these challenges, SPACs remain an important innovation within capital markets because they expanded the strategic options available to private companies. In many cases, SPACs enabled businesses to secure capital and public visibility that may not have been possible through traditional methods. They also demonstrated how financial markets continually evolve to accommodate changing economic conditions, technological innovation, and investor demand.

SPACs are not the only alternative path to becoming public. Reverse mergers also represent an important strategy within the world of alternative public offerings. In a reverse merger, a private company merges with an existing publicly traded company, often one with minimal operations. Through this transaction, the private company effectively gains public listing status. Reverse mergers have existed for many years and have been used by companies seeking faster or less expensive access to public markets. Direct listings provide another alternative approach. In a direct listing, a company allows existing shareholders to sell shares directly to the public without issuing new shares or relying heavily on traditional underwriters. This approach can reduce underwriting costs and avoid dilution from issuing additional shares. Companies with strong brand recognition and sufficient financial resources sometimes choose direct listings because they do not necessarily need to raise new capital immediately.

The evolution of alternative public offerings reflects a broader shift within the global economy. Entrepreneurship has become increasingly decentralized and technology-driven. Startups can scale globally at unprecedented speeds. Investors seek exposure to innovation earlier in the growth cycle. Public markets themselves have become more accessible through digital trading platforms and online investing communities. These changes have created demand for more flexible capital-raising mechanisms.

Understanding SPACs also requires understanding investor psychology. Public market valuations are influenced not only by financial performance but also by narratives, expectations, market momentum, and future growth potential. Investors often become highly enthusiastic about disruptive technologies and visionary founders. During periods of speculative optimism, valuations can rise dramatically even before companies achieve profitability. While this can create extraordinary wealth, it can also produce extreme volatility.

One of the most fascinating aspects of SPACs is how they blend finance, entrepreneurship, marketing, and storytelling. Successful SPAC transactions often depend on a compelling growth narrative supported by credible leadership and scalable business models. Investors must believe not only in current operations but also in the company's long-term vision. This creates a unique environment where perception and execution become deeply interconnected.

As alternative public offerings continue evolving, entrepreneurs must think strategically about which path best aligns with their business objectives. A traditional IPO may offer prestige and institutional credibility. A SPAC merger may provide speed and pricing certainty. A direct listing may reduce dilution. A reverse merger may offer simplicity. Each option carries trade-offs involving cost, control, valuation, regulatory complexity, and long-term shareholder dynamics.

The future of public markets will likely involve continued experimentation and innovation. Financial technology, blockchain systems, tokenized securities, global crowdfunding platforms, and digital assets may eventually create entirely new methods for companies to raise capital and access liquidity. The rise of SPACs demonstrated that even long-established financial systems can evolve rapidly when market demand shifts. For founders, investors, and financial professionals, understanding these developments is essential. Public markets remain one of the most powerful engines of wealth creation in modern history. Companies that successfully access capital, scale operations, and maintain investor confidence can create enormous value for shareholders, employees, and founders alike. However, achieving long-term success requires more than simply becoming public. It requires disciplined leadership, operational excellence, strategic vision, and the ability to adapt to changing market conditions.

Alternative public offerings are not shortcuts to guaranteed success. They are financial tools that can accelerate opportunity when used correctly but can also magnify weaknesses when poorly executed. Entrepreneurs must understand both the opportunities and responsibilities associated with entering the public markets. Investors must evaluate transactions carefully and avoid becoming overly influenced by hype or speculation.

Ultimately, the rise of SPACs and alternative listing strategies represents a new chapter in the evolution of capitalism and entrepreneurship. These structures reflect a world where innovation moves faster, capital flows more globally, and companies seek increasingly flexible methods to achieve growth and liquidity. Understanding how these systems work provides valuable insight into the future of business, investing, and long-term wealth creation.

The Fast Track to Wall Street

Ethan Ramirez stared at the glowing city skyline from the conference room window as rain slid slowly down the glass. Below him, Manhattan moved with its usual relentless pace. Yellow taxis flowed through intersections like currents in a river, while thousands of office lights flickered across the financial district. At thirty-six years old, Ethan had built one of the fastest-growing artificial intelligence logistics companies in the country. Yet despite the headlines, investor meetings, and rapid expansion, he faced a problem that threatened everything he had built.

His company, VelocityGrid AI, had grown from a small startup operating out of a rented warehouse in Miami into a national logistics software platform used by major shipping companies and retailers. The business used artificial intelligence to optimize delivery routes, warehouse operations, and inventory forecasting. Revenue had tripled within two years, but scaling the company further required capital far beyond what traditional private investors were willing to provide.

"We're reaching the limit," said his CFO, Rebecca Lin, sitting across the conference table. "We need serious expansion capital if we want to compete globally." Ethan nodded quietly. He already knew the numbers. The company needed hundreds of millions of dollars to continue expanding infrastructure, hiring engineers, and securing international partnerships. Competitors were moving aggressively. Venture capital firms wanted greater ownership control. Traditional bank financing would not provide nearly enough liquidity.

"What about a traditional IPO?" Ethan asked.

Rebecca exhaled slowly. "Possible, but it could take over a year. Audits, roadshows, underwriters, SEC reviews, market timing. And honestly, the market's unstable right now."

Ethan turned back toward the skyline. Every day mattered. The artificial intelligence sector was exploding with competition. Waiting another year could mean losing market leadership entirely.

Two weeks later, Ethan found himself seated inside a private conference room overlooking Central Park. Across from him sat Jonathan Pierce, a former hedge fund manager turned SPAC sponsor. Pierce had recently launched Apex Future Holdings, a Special Purpose Acquisition Company with nearly $500 million in capital searching for an acquisition target in the technology sector.

Jonathan leaned forward confidently. "Ethan, your company is exactly the type of business we're looking for. High-growth industry, scalable technology, recurring revenue, strong management team."

Ethan listened carefully. He had spent the previous week researching SPACs intensely. Some deals had created billionaires almost overnight. Others had collapsed spectacularly.

"What's the real advantage here?" Ethan asked directly.

"Speed," Jonathan replied immediately. "A traditional IPO could take twelve to eighteen months. We can potentially bring you public within six."

Rebecca, who sat beside Ethan, added cautiously, "And valuation certainty."

Jonathan smiled. "Exactly. We negotiate the valuation directly. No last-minute underwriter surprises."

Over the next several months, negotiations intensified. Attorneys, accountants, bankers, consultants, and analysts filled endless virtual meetings discussing financial projections, ownership structures, PIPE financing, and shareholder approvals. Ethan quickly realized that going public involved far more complexity than simply raising money.

Late one evening, Ethan sat alone in his Miami office reviewing dilution scenarios. His ownership percentage would decrease significantly after the merger. PIPE investors wanted discounted shares. The SPAC sponsors held founder shares that added further dilution. Yet despite the compromises, the transaction would provide enough capital to transform VelocityGrid into a global competitor.

As news of the potential merger leaked online, investor excitement exploded. Financial media outlets described VelocityGrid as "the future of AI-powered logistics." Retail investors flooded online forums discussing the company's potential. Analysts began publishing speculative price targets before the merger had even closed.

Ethan watched the frenzy with mixed emotions. Part of him felt proud. Another part felt deeply uneasy. The company was becoming a public narrative, not just a business.

His concerns grew after attending investor marketing presentations in New York. Some presentations projected extraordinary growth rates extending ten years into the future. Others compared VelocityGrid to massive technology giants despite the company still operating at relatively modest scale.

After one particularly aggressive investor meeting, Ethan confronted Jonathan privately.

"Some of these projections are insane," Ethan said firmly.

Jonathan shrugged calmly. "Welcome to public markets."

"But what happens if we don't hit these numbers?"

Jonathan paused. "Then the market adjusts."

The merger eventually closed successfully. VelocityGrid officially became publicly traded on the Nasdaq under the ticker symbol VGAI. On the first day of trading, the company's valuation surged beyond $3 billion.

Ethan stood on the Nasdaq stage during the opening bell ceremony while cameras flashed around him. Employees cheered. Investors celebrated. Financial reporters crowded around the executives asking questions about the future of artificial intelligence and global expansion.

For a moment, Ethan felt unstoppable.

The capital influx transformed the company almost overnight. VelocityGrid opened new offices internationally, hired hundreds of engineers, acquired smaller competitors, and signed major partnerships with retailers and transportation companies. Ethan's personal net worth skyrocketed into the hundreds of millions on paper.

But public markets brought new pressures Ethan had not fully anticipated. Quarterly earnings calls became brutal examinations of every financial metric. Analysts questioned revenue growth rates, customer acquisition costs, and profit margins. Social media amplified every rumor and disappointment. Online traders celebrated the stock one week and attacked it the next.

Then came the market downturn.

Interest rates rose sharply. Growth stocks collapsed across the technology sector. Investor sentiment shifted dramatically. Companies that had once been praised for aggressive expansion were suddenly criticized for lacking profitability.

VelocityGrid's stock price fell more than sixty percent within eight months.

Financial media outlets that once praised Ethan now questioned whether SPAC-era valuations had become dangerously inflated. Short sellers published reports criticizing the company's growth assumptions. Employees worried about layoffs as the stock continued declining.

One evening, Ethan sat alone again in his office overlooking Miami Beach. The excitement of the Nasdaq opening bell felt distant now. The public markets had transformed his life financially, but they had also exposed him to enormous pressure, scrutiny, and volatility. Rebecca entered quietly carrying updated financial reports.

"We still have strong cash reserves," she said carefully. "Operationally, we're stable."

Ethan nodded silently.

"The market may be punishing us," Rebecca continued, "but the business itself is real."

That statement stayed with Ethan for months.

Gradually, he began shifting his focus away from stock price volatility and back toward operational fundamentals. The company reduced unnecessary spending, improved profitability, strengthened client retention, and focused on sustainable long-term growth instead of aggressive market hype.

Over the next three years, VelocityGrid slowly rebuilt investor confidence. Revenue stabilized. Profit margins improved. Institutional investors returned. The company expanded strategically instead of recklessly.

By the company's fifth anniversary as a public entity, VelocityGrid had evolved into one of the leading logistics AI companies globally. Ethan had learned one of the most important lessons in capital markets: going public can create wealth quickly, but maintaining that wealth requires discipline, execution, adaptability, and resilience.

During an interview at an entrepreneurship conference years later, a young founder asked Ethan whether taking the company public through a SPAC had been the right decision.

Ethan smiled thoughtfully before answering.

"The SPAC didn't create the company," he said. "It simply accelerated the opportunity. What mattered afterward was whether we could actually build a real business capable of surviving public markets."

The audience remained silent as he continued.

"A lot of people think becoming public is the finish line. It's not. It's the beginning of a much harder game."

Understanding the mechanics of a SPAC transaction is essential for anyone interested in modern capital markets, entrepreneurship, startup finance, or alternative public offerings. While SPACs may initially seem complicated due to their legal structures, financial terminology, and regulatory processes, the underlying concept is relatively straightforward once broken down into stages. A SPAC transaction essentially allows a private company to become publicly traded through a merger with an already-public shell company that was specifically created for that purpose. However, behind this seemingly simple concept lies a highly sophisticated process involving investors, sponsors, attorneys, regulators, accountants, investment bankers, and corporate executives.

To understand how SPAC transactions work, it is important to first examine the creation of the SPAC itself. A SPAC begins with a group of sponsors who decide to form a publicly traded acquisition company. These sponsors are usually experienced investors, private equity professionals, hedge fund managers, former corporate executives, venture capitalists, or individuals with deep expertise in a particular industry. Their goal is to

Chapter 2

How SPAC Transactions Work Step by Step

Understanding the mechanics of a SPAC transaction is essential for anyone interested in modern capital markets, entrepreneurship, startup finance, or alternative public offerings. While SPACs may initially appear complicated due to their legal structures, financial terminology, and regulatory processes, the underlying concept is relatively straightforward once broken down into stages. A SPAC transaction essentially allows a private company to become publicly traded through a merger with an already-public shell company that was specifically created for that purpose. However, behind this seemingly simple concept lies a highly sophisticated process involving investors, sponsors, attorneys, regulators, accountants, investment bankers, and corporate executives.

To understand how SPAC transactions work, it is important to first examine the creation of the SPAC itself. A SPAC begins with a group of sponsors who decide to form a publicly traded acquisition company. These sponsors are usually experienced investors, private equity professionals, hedge fund managers, former corporate executives, venture capitalists, or individuals with deep expertise in a particular industry. Their goal is to raise money from public investors and then identify a promising private company to acquire or merge with in the future.

The sponsors create the SPAC entity and contribute initial capital, often referred to as "at-risk capital," to cover organizational expenses, legal fees, underwriting costs, and administrative operations. In exchange for this early financial commitment, the sponsors typically receive founder shares that may later convert into a significant ownership stake after the merger is completed. This ownership structure is one of the defining characteristics of SPACs and also one of the most debated aspects of the model because it can create dilution for future shareholders.

After forming the SPAC entity, the sponsors work with investment banks to conduct the SPAC's own initial public offering. Unlike a traditional operating company IPO, the SPAC itself has no active business operations. Investors purchasing shares in the SPAC are essentially investing in the sponsors' ability to identify and complete a successful acquisition. This means investor confidence often depends heavily on the reputation, experience, and track record of the sponsor team.

During the SPAC IPO, units are sold to investors, usually at a standard price such as ten dollars per unit. Each unit commonly includes one share of stock along with a fraction of a warrant, which gives investors the right to purchase additional shares later at a specified price. These warrants are designed to make the investment more attractive by offering potential upside if the eventual merger succeeds.

The money raised during the SPAC IPO is placed into a trust account and invested in relatively safe securities such as U.S. Treasury instruments. Importantly, the SPAC sponsors generally cannot access these funds freely. The capital is reserved for the future acquisition transaction or returned to investors if no merger occurs within the required timeframe.

Once the SPAC completes its IPO, the search phase begins. Sponsors usually have a limited period, often around eighteen to twenty-four months, to identify and complete a merger with a private company. This time pressure creates urgency because failure to complete a transaction within the allotted timeframe can force the SPAC to liquidate and return investor funds.

During the search process, SPAC sponsors evaluate numerous private companies based on factors such as industry growth potential, revenue trends, scalability, profitability, management quality, competitive advantages, market positioning, and investor appeal. Sponsors typically seek businesses with compelling narratives that can attract public market enthusiasm. High-growth sectors such as artificial intelligence, electric vehicles, biotechnology, renewable energy, fintech, cybersecurity, and digital platforms often become major targets because investors are drawn to industries with perceived future expansion opportunities.

Once a promising target company is identified, negotiations begin. One of the major advantages of SPAC transactions is that valuation negotiations occur privately between the SPAC sponsors and the target company management team. Unlike traditional IPOs where pricing is finalized near the public offering date based on market demand, SPAC mergers allow both sides to establish valuation terms earlier in the process. This can create greater certainty for founders and early investors regarding ownership outcomes.

The negotiation process involves extensive financial analysis, legal due diligence, and operational review. Auditors examine financial statements. Attorneys review contracts, intellectual property, regulatory exposure, and litigation risks. Investment bankers analyze market comparables and valuation models. Sponsors attempt to determine whether the company can realistically succeed as a publicly traded enterprise.

After preliminary agreements are reached, the SPAC publicly announces the proposed merger transaction. This announcement often generates significant investor attention because it finally reveals the private company that investors are effectively backing. Stock prices may rise dramatically if the market views the target company positively. Media coverage, analyst commentary, and online investor discussions frequently intensify following the announcement.

At this stage, the SPAC and target company begin preparing detailed regulatory filings for the Securities and Exchange Commission. These filings disclose financial information, business risks, operational details, management backgrounds, merger structures, and future projections. Public shareholders must receive sufficient information to evaluate whether they approve of the proposed transaction.

One feature that made SPAC transactions especially attractive to growth-stage companies was the ability to present forward-looking financial projections more openly than in traditional IPOs. Many companies used ambitious revenue forecasts and long-term growth estimates to justify high valuations. While this flexibility generated excitement, it also contributed to unrealistic expectations in some cases. Investors eventually learned that projections alone do not guarantee successful execution.

Another critical component of many SPAC transactions is PIPE financing, which stands for Private Investment in Public Equity. PIPE investors are typically institutional investors, hedge funds, mutual funds, or private equity firms that agree to invest additional capital into the transaction alongside the SPAC merger. PIPE financing serves several purposes. It increases the amount of cash available to the merged company, strengthens market confidence, and helps offset potential investor redemptions.

Investor redemptions represent one of the most important risks within SPAC transactions. SPAC shareholders generally have the right to redeem their shares and receive cash from the trust account before the merger closes if they do not support the proposed deal. High redemption rates can significantly reduce the amount of capital available to the merged company and may even threaten the viability of the transaction itself.

For this reason, SPAC sponsors and target company executives spend substantial effort marketing the transaction to investors. Investor presentations, media appearances, conference calls, and analyst discussions become critical tools for maintaining confidence. The company must convince shareholders that the proposed merger creates long-term value and justifies continued investment.

After regulatory reviews are completed and shareholder votes occur, the merger officially closes. This stage is commonly referred to as the "de-SPAC" process because the private company effectively replaces the SPAC shell entity and begins operating as a publicly traded company. The company's shares begin trading publicly under a new ticker symbol, and the former private business officially enters the public markets.

At this moment, many founders experience a dramatic financial transformation. Shares that were once privately held become publicly tradable assets with observable market valuations. Employees holding stock options may suddenly possess significant wealth on paper. Early investors may achieve liquidity opportunities that were previously unavailable in private markets.

However, becoming public introduces entirely new responsibilities and pressures. Public companies must comply with quarterly reporting requirements, SEC regulations, governance standards, investor communications, and market expectations. Management teams become accountable not only to private investors but also to public shareholders, analysts, regulators, and institutional investors.

One of the most challenging aspects of post-merger life is managing public market expectations. During bullish market periods, investors often reward aggressive growth narratives and optimistic forecasts. But when economic conditions weaken or companies fail to meet projections, stock prices can decline rapidly. Many SPAC-era companies experienced extreme volatility because investor enthusiasm shifted dramatically once operational realities became clearer.

Some companies that entered public markets through SPACs performed exceptionally well. They used public capital effectively, expanded operations, improved profitability, and delivered long-term shareholder value. Others struggled with execution problems, unrealistic valuations, operational inefficiencies, or declining investor confidence. These outcomes demonstrated that while SPACs may accelerate access to public markets, they do not eliminate the fundamental challenges of building sustainable businesses.

Critics of SPACs often point to dilution, conflicts of interest, and speculative behavior as weaknesses within the structure. Sponsors may benefit financially even if long-term shareholder performance disappoints. Retail investors sometimes enter transactions late after valuations have already become inflated. Aggressive marketing campaigns and social media hype can distort investor expectations.

Supporters, however, argue that SPACs provide valuable flexibility within capital markets. They allow innovative companies to raise capital more efficiently, create liquidity opportunities, and access public investors without relying entirely on traditional IPO structures. SPACs also demonstrate that financial markets are capable of evolving in response to changing economic environments and technological innovation.

The rise of SPACs reflected broader trends within modern entrepreneurship and investing. Startups increasingly operate in industries where speed matters enormously. Companies often seek rapid expansion in winner-take-all markets where securing capital quickly can determine competitive survival. Investors also seek exposure to high-growth industries earlier in the business lifecycle.

Understanding SPAC transactions requires understanding incentives. Sponsors seek profitable acquisitions. Founders seek capital and liquidity. Investors seek growth opportunities. Investment banks seek underwriting and advisory fees. PIPE investors seek discounted investments with upside potential. Regulators seek investor protection and market transparency. These overlapping incentives shape how transactions are structured and negotiated.

Another important lesson is that financial engineering alone cannot create lasting business success. A SPAC merger may provide capital, visibility, and market access, but long-term performance still depends on execution, profitability, operational scalability, and leadership quality. Public markets eventually demand results beyond projections and narratives.

As financial markets continue evolving, SPACs may remain an important part of the capital-raising ecosystem even if market enthusiasm fluctuates over time. New regulatory standards, improved governance practices, and more disciplined valuation methods may strengthen future transactions. Entrepreneurs and investors who understand how these structures work will be better positioned to evaluate opportunities intelligently.

Ultimately, SPAC transactions represent more than just financial structures. They reflect a broader transformation in how companies raise capital, how investors access growth opportunities, and how wealth can be created through innovation and public market participation. By understanding the full transaction process step by step, readers gain valuable insight into one of the most influential financial developments of the modern era.

The Merger Deadline

Sophia Bennett sat alone inside the dimly lit conference room at midnight, staring at the massive digital countdown displayed on the presentation screen. Twenty-one days remained before the SPAC merger deadline expired. Outside the glass walls of the office tower, Chicago glowed beneath a cold winter storm. Snow drifted through the city streets while traffic crawled slowly below. Inside the office, however, the atmosphere felt far more dangerous than the weather outside.

Her company, NexaVolt Energy Systems, had spent six years developing advanced battery storage technology for renewable energy grids. What began as a university research project had evolved into one of the fastest-growing clean energy startups in North America. Major utility companies were testing NexaVolt's systems, and investors believed the technology could transform how renewable energy was stored and distributed globally.

But success had come at a cost.

The company was burning through cash rapidly. Manufacturing expansion required hundreds of millions of dollars. Competitors backed by massive venture capital firms were entering the market aggressively. Traditional financing options had become increasingly limited after rising interest rates weakened investor appetite for speculative growth companies.

Then came Titan Horizon Acquisition Corp., a SPAC led by billionaire investor Michael Halpern. At first, the deal seemed perfect. Titan Horizon had raised over $600 million in its SPAC IPO and specifically targeted renewable energy companies. Halpern's reputation alone generated enormous excitement throughout Wall Street. Financial media outlets described him as one of the most influential investors in sustainable infrastructure.

When Titan Horizon approached NexaVolt with a proposed merger, Sophia initially hesitated. She had heard stories about SPAC deals collapsing after inflated projections failed to materialize. But after months of negotiations, the opportunity appeared impossible to ignore.

The merger would value NexaVolt at nearly $3.2 billion.

The capital infusion would fund manufacturing facilities, international expansion, research laboratories, and strategic acquisitions. Employees holding stock options could become multimillionaires overnight.

Yet now, with only three weeks remaining before the shareholder vote, the entire transaction was unraveling.

"We have a redemption problem," said Daniel Reeves, NexaVolt's CFO, as he entered the conference room carrying updated reports.

Sophia rubbed her eyes tiredly. "How bad?"

Daniel placed the documents on the table.

"Potentially catastrophic."

She scanned the numbers silently. Nearly seventy percent of SPAC shareholders were considering redeeming their shares instead of participating in the merger.

"That would destroy the trust capital," Sophia whispered.

Daniel nodded grimly. "Without enough remaining cash, we may violate minimum funding requirements."

The situation reflected broader market panic. Over the previous six months, investor sentiment toward SPACs had deteriorated dramatically. Rising interest rates, disappointing earnings from previously merged companies, and regulatory scrutiny had triggered widespread fear throughout the market.

Many investors no longer trusted aggressive growth projections.

And NexaVolt's projections were aggressive.

The company forecasted revenue growth exceeding 400% within four years based on expected renewable energy adoption trends. Analysts questioned whether the manufacturing scale-up could realistically occur that quickly.

The next morning, Sophia flew to New York for emergency meetings with Titan Horizon executives and PIPE investors.

Inside a luxury Manhattan boardroom overlooking Central Park, tensions filled the air.

"We need stronger institutional support," Michael Halpern said firmly. "If redemption levels stay this high, the deal becomes unstable."

One of the investment bankers leaned forward cautiously. "Several PIPE investors are requesting revised valuation terms."

Sophia felt frustration rising inside her.

"They want lower prices now?" she asked sharply.

"They're concerned about market conditions," the banker replied diplomatically.

Sophia looked around the room. Months earlier, everyone had praised NexaVolt as the future of clean energy infrastructure.

Now those same investors suddenly questioned whether the company deserved its valuation.

Fear had replaced optimism.

That afternoon, Sophia participated in a live investor webcast designed to rebuild confidence. Thousands of retail investors watched online while institutional analysts submitted questions about revenue forecasts, supply chain risks, profitability timelines, and competitive pressures.

One analyst asked bluntly, "Why should investors trust these projections when so many SPAC companies have missed expectations recently?"

Sophia paused before answering.

"Because unlike many companies built around speculation, we already have signed commercial contracts, operational technology, and real customer demand," she replied calmly.

But privately, she knew confidence alone would not save the transaction.

Over the following two weeks, negotiations intensified around the clock.

PIPE investors demanded additional protections. Attorneys revised merger terms repeatedly. Accountants updated forecasts daily. Public relations firms launched media campaigns emphasizing NexaVolt's long-term growth potential.

Meanwhile, social media investors debated the deal aggressively online. Some viewed NexaVolt as a revolutionary clean energy company poised for massive expansion. Others described it as another overhyped SPAC destined for collapse.

Sophia barely slept.

Late one evening, she sat alone in her hotel room staring at financial models covering the desk. She thought back to the early days of the company when she and two engineers worked from a small rented warehouse with almost no funding.

Back then, survival depended on solving engineering problems.

Now survival depended on managing capital markets psychology.

The final shareholder vote arrived on a freezing January morning.

Inside the Nasdaq conference center, executives, bankers, attorneys, and investors waited anxiously as redemption numbers updated in real time.

At first, the numbers looked disastrous.

Forty percent redeemed.

Then fifty percent.

Sophia felt her stomach tighten. But unexpectedly, several major institutional investors increased their PIPE commitments at the final hour after securing revised terms. The additional capital stabilized the deal.

By late afternoon, Titan Horizon officially approved the merger.

NexaVolt became publicly traded under the ticker NVXS.

Employees erupted in celebration.

Financial media outlets announced the transaction across global headlines. Sophia appeared on multiple television interviews discussing the future of renewable energy infrastructure.

For a brief moment, everything felt victorious.

Then public trading began.

The stock surged initially before collapsing nearly thirty percent within two weeks as volatility consumed the broader market. Retail traders moved in and out rapidly. Short sellers targeted clean energy SPAC companies aggressively.

Public market life proved far harsher than private fundraising.

Quarterly earnings pressure intensified. Investors demanded faster profitability. Analysts questioned every operational setback. Manufacturing delays triggered brutal stock selloffs.

Sophia gradually realized that going public had not solved the company's challenges. It had amplified them. But unlike many SPAC-era companies, NexaVolt possessed one major advantage: real operational demand.

Over the next several years, renewable energy adoption accelerated globally. Utility contracts expanded. Battery storage infrastructure became increasingly essential to energy grids worldwide.

Slowly, the company stabilized.

Revenue growth became real instead of speculative. Profitability improved. Institutional investors returned. The stock recovered steadily as the business matured operationally.

Five years later, Sophia stood once again inside Nasdaq's headquarters preparing for another interview.

A young entrepreneur approached her afterward.

"Was the SPAC worth it?" he asked.

Sophia smiled thoughtfully.

"The SPAC gave us access to capital," she replied. "But surviving public markets required something much harder."

"What was that?"

She looked toward the trading floor below before answering.

"Building a company strong enough to survive after the excitement disappears."

Chapter 3

The Advantages and Risks of SPACs for Founders and Investors

The rise of Special Purpose Acquisition Companies dramatically reshaped the conversation surrounding public market access, startup financing, wealth creation, and modern entrepreneurship. For some companies, SPAC mergers created transformative opportunities that accelerated growth, unlocked billions in capital, and generated life-changing wealth for founders, employees, and investors. For others, SPAC transactions became cautionary examples of inflated expectations, weak execution, excessive speculation, and public market volatility. Understanding both the advantages and risks of SPACs is essential for anyone seeking to navigate modern capital markets intelligently.

Every financial structure carries trade-offs. SPACs are no exception. While they provide faster and often more flexible alternatives to traditional IPOs, they also introduce unique risks related to valuation, dilution, governance, investor psychology, and long-term operational performance. Founders considering SPAC transactions must carefully evaluate whether the structure aligns with their business goals, financial position, and growth strategy. Investors must similarly understand the incentives, mechanics, and potential vulnerabilities within these deals before committing capital.

One of the greatest advantages of a SPAC transaction for founders is speed. Traditional IPOs can take many months or even years to complete. Companies must undergo extensive audits, prepare registration statements, coordinate with underwriters, conduct investor roadshows, and navigate regulatory reviews. Market conditions can shift dramatically during this period, potentially delaying or weakening the offering. In contrast, SPAC mergers can often move much more quickly because the SPAC itself has already completed its own IPO and is already publicly traded.

For fast-growing companies operating in highly competitive industries, speed can provide enormous strategic value. Technology markets evolve rapidly. Consumer behavior changes quickly. Competitive advantages can disappear if companies fail to scale efficiently. Accessing public capital faster may allow businesses to hire talent, expand internationally, increase marketing efforts, acquire competitors, and invest in research before rivals capture market share. In industries driven by innovation, timing can significantly influence long-term success. Another major advantage involves valuation certainty. In a traditional IPO, pricing often occurs near the final offering date and depends heavily on investor demand, market sentiment, and underwriter negotiations. Companies sometimes feel frustrated when strong demand causes stocks to surge after the IPO, suggesting the shares may have been initially underpriced. SPAC mergers allow companies and sponsors to negotiate valuations privately ahead of time. This creates more predictability regarding ownership percentages, capital proceeds, and post-transaction structures.

For founders and early investors, this valuation certainty can be highly attractive. Entrepreneurs often spend years building businesses and may prefer negotiating directly with experienced sponsors rather than depending entirely on shifting public market conditions during IPO pricing. SPAC negotiations can also create opportunities to structure transactions creatively based on the company's long-term growth plans and strategic objectives.

SPACs also offer broader access to public capital markets for companies that may not fit the traditional IPO model. Many emerging industries involve companies with limited profitability, short operating histories, or highly innovative business models that traditional IPO investors may initially hesitate to support. SPACs became particularly popular among companies in sectors such as electric vehicles, artificial intelligence, renewable energy, biotechnology, fintech, space exploration, and digital platforms because investors were eager to participate in future-oriented growth opportunities.

Another important advantage involves marketing flexibility. Historically, SPAC mergers allowed companies to present forward-looking financial projections more openly than traditional IPOs. This enabled companies to communicate ambitious growth strategies and long-term market opportunities directly to investors. Founders could emphasize future revenue potential, technological disruption, scalability, and industry transformation rather than focusing exclusively on historical financial performance.

For visionary entrepreneurs, this flexibility created opportunities to attract investor enthusiasm around innovation and future expansion. Companies with strong narratives often generated substantial media attention, retail investor interest, and institutional capital inflows. In some cases, SPAC transactions created massive public visibility for companies that previously operated relatively quietly in private markets.

Liquidity also represents a major benefit for founders, employees, and early investors. Private company ownership can create significant paper wealth, but liquidity may remain limited until an exit event occurs. A SPAC merger allows shares to become publicly tradable, potentially enabling founders and investors to realize gains from years of work and investment. Employees holding stock options may suddenly possess valuable financial assets that can transform their personal lives.

Public company status may also enhance credibility and strategic flexibility. Publicly traded companies often gain greater visibility with customers, suppliers, lenders, institutional investors, and strategic partners. Public stock can also serve as acquisition currency for purchasing other businesses. In highly competitive industries, public market access can strengthen a company's overall market position significantly.

Despite these advantages, SPAC transactions carry substantial risks that both founders and investors must understand carefully. One of the most significant concerns involves dilution. SPAC sponsors typically receive founder shares, often called the "promote," which can represent a considerable ownership stake after the merger closes. Additional dilution may arise through warrants, PIPE financing, convertible securities, and employee compensation structures.

For founders, dilution can reduce long-term ownership percentages more than initially anticipated. While access to capital may justify some dilution, poorly structured deals can leave founders with significantly less control or economic upside than expected. Investors must similarly understand how dilution affects earnings potential, voting rights, and future shareholder value.

Another major risk involves unrealistic valuations. During periods of market optimism, some SPAC-era companies achieved valuations based more on speculative future projections than current operational performance. Companies promising revolutionary technologies or disruptive growth often attracted extraordinary investor enthusiasm despite limited revenues or unproven business models. When actual results failed to meet expectations, stock prices sometimes collapsed dramatically.

This disconnect between projections and reality created severe consequences for many investors. Retail investors entering transactions late often purchased shares at inflated prices during periods of excitement and momentum. Once market sentiment shifted or operational challenges emerged, losses could become substantial. The SPAC boom demonstrated how investor psychology, media narratives, and speculative behavior can temporarily distort valuations far beyond fundamental business performance.

Public market pressure represents another major challenge for founders. Many entrepreneurs excel at innovation, product development, and private company growth but struggle with the demands of operating a public company. Quarterly earnings expectations, analyst scrutiny, shareholder activism, media attention, regulatory compliance, and stock price volatility can create intense pressure on management teams.

Founders who once focused primarily on long-term strategy may suddenly face constant short-term performance expectations from public investors. Public companies must communicate regularly with shareholders while maintaining operational discipline and financial transparency. Leadership mistakes, missed projections, or negative headlines can trigger immediate stock price declines and reputational damage.

Investor redemptions also create unique risks within SPAC transactions. SPAC shareholders generally have the right to redeem their shares before the merger closes if they dislike the proposed deal. High redemption rates can dramatically reduce available cash and weaken the financial stability of the merged company. In some cases, companies expecting large capital inflows received far less funding than anticipated because shareholders redeemed aggressively.

This redemption risk became particularly severe during periods when investor confidence in SPACs weakened broadly. As market conditions deteriorated, many investors chose redemption over continued participation, forcing companies to secure additional financing or renegotiate transaction terms. Companies dependent on specific capital amounts for expansion plans faced significant operational challenges when funding fell short.

Regulatory scrutiny increased substantially as SPAC activity accelerated. Financial regulators became concerned about accounting standards, disclosure quality, conflicts of interest, overly optimistic projections, and investor protection issues. Several companies faced investigations or lawsuits related to misleading statements, inaccurate forecasts, or inadequate disclosures following SPAC mergers.

These regulatory pressures highlighted the importance of transparency, governance, and realistic communication with investors. Companies entering public markets through SPACs learned that financial engineering alone could not replace operational execution or sound corporate management.

Another important risk involves market timing. SPAC transactions often flourish during bullish market periods characterized by low interest rates, abundant liquidity, and strong investor appetite for speculative growth opportunities. However, when economic conditions shift, investor behavior can change rapidly. Rising interest rates, inflation concerns, geopolitical instability, or economic slowdowns may reduce investor enthusiasm for high-growth companies with uncertain profitability.

This cyclical nature of capital markets means that companies entering public markets during euphoric periods may later face sharp valuation corrections if broader market sentiment deteriorates. Founders and investors must recognize that external economic conditions can strongly influence public company performance regardless of operational quality.

For investors, evaluating SPAC opportunities requires careful analysis beyond promotional narratives. Investors should examine management quality, industry trends, financial statements, competitive positioning, customer demand, scalability, governance practices, and realistic valuation assumptions. Blindly following hype or celebrity sponsorship without understanding business fundamentals can lead to significant losses.

At the same time, SPACs are not inherently negative or dangerous structures. Like any financial tool, their effectiveness depends on how they are used. Some companies that entered public markets through SPACs became highly successful businesses with strong operational performance and long-term shareholder returns. Others failed because their underlying business models were weak, their projections unrealistic, or their execution insufficient.

The SPAC era also revealed broader truths about modern financial markets. Public markets increasingly reward narratives around innovation, disruption, scalability, and future growth potential. Technology and social media accelerate information flow, investor enthusiasm, and market momentum at unprecedented speeds. Retail investor participation has expanded dramatically through digital trading platforms and online investing communities. These changes have created both extraordinary opportunities and heightened volatility.

Founders considering SPAC transactions must therefore think carefully about their readiness for public life. Becoming publicly traded can provide enormous advantages, but it also requires financial discipline, operational maturity, governance systems, investor relations capabilities, and long-term strategic planning. Public markets reward execution over time, not merely initial excitement.

Investors must similarly develop discipline and critical

thinking. Successful investing requires evaluating risk realistically, understanding market psychology, and distinguishing between compelling narratives and sustainable businesses. Wealth creation in public markets often comes not from chasing short-term hype but from identifying companies capable of delivering long-term operational success.

The evolution of SPACs ultimately reflects the changing nature of entrepreneurship, investing, and capital formation in the modern economy. Innovation moves faster. Capital flows globally. Investors seek earlier access to growth opportunities. Companies demand greater flexibility in raising funds and accessing liquidity. SPACs emerged because they addressed these evolving needs, even if the structure itself remains imperfect.

As capital markets continue evolving, SPACs may remain one important option among many for companies seeking public market access. Future regulatory reforms, improved governance standards, and more disciplined valuation practices may strengthen the structure further. Entrepreneurs and investors who understand both the opportunities and risks will be better prepared to navigate this evolving financial landscape intelligently.

Ultimately, SPACs represent neither guaranteed wealth

machines nor inherently flawed financial structures. They are tools that can accelerate opportunity when combined with strong businesses, capable leadership, disciplined execution, and realistic expectations. Understanding both their advantages and their dangers provides valuable insight into the future of public markets and long-term wealth creation.

The Billion-Dollar Illusion

Marcus Holloway stood backstage behind the massive conference curtains, listening to the roar of applause echo through the auditorium. Thousands of investors, analysts, media reporters, and technology enthusiasts filled the Las Vegas convention center waiting for him to take the stage.

Above the audience, enormous digital screens displayed the logo of QuantumDrive Robotics, the autonomous trucking startup Marcus founded only four years earlier.

The company had become one of the hottest names in the SPAC boom.

And according to Wall Street, Marcus was now worth nearly two billion dollars.

At thirty-four years old, he had gone from sleeping on a friend's couch to appearing on financial television networks discussing the future of artificial intelligence and transportation automation. Investors described him as a visionary entrepreneur capable of disrupting the trillion-dollar logistics industry. But beneath the excitement, Marcus carried a growing sense of anxiety he could no longer ignore.

Three years earlier, QuantumDrive operated from a small warehouse outside Phoenix. Marcus and a team of engineers worked endlessly to develop autonomous freight software designed to reduce trucking costs and improve delivery efficiency.

The technology showed promise, but the company struggled financially. Competitors with larger funding rounds moved aggressively into the market. Manufacturing hardware prototypes required enormous capital. Traditional venture investors demanded substantial ownership control in exchange for additional financing.

Then came Nova Capital Acquisition Corp., a SPAC led by former private equity executive Richard Kane.

Richard approached Marcus with what seemed like the opportunity of a lifetime.

"We can take QuantumDrive public within six months," Richard explained during their first meeting in Miami. "You'll gain access to hundreds of millions in expansion capital immediately."

Marcus initially hesitated. He knew little about SPACs.

But as negotiations progressed, the numbers became impossible to ignore.

The proposed merger valued QuantumDrive at $4.8 billion despite the company generating less than $30 million in annual revenue.

"We're valuing future dominance," Richard said confidently.

Investment banks created presentations forecasting explosive revenue growth over the next decade. Analysts described autonomous freight systems as inevitable. Media outlets praised QuantumDrive as "the Tesla of trucking."

Suddenly, everyone wanted access to the deal.

Retail investors flooded online forums discussing QuantumDrive's future. Social media influencers promoted the stock aggressively. Financial television networks invited Marcus for interviews almost weekly.

During one television appearance, the host smiled excitedly.

"Do you believe QuantumDrive could become a $100 billion company one day?"

Marcus hesitated briefly before answering carefully.

"We believe autonomous logistics will transform global transportation."

The host grinned. "That sounds like a yes."

Investor enthusiasm intensified further after the merger officially closed.

QuantumDrive began trading publicly under the ticker QDRV.

On its first trading day, the stock surged nearly eighty percent.

Marcus watched the numbers update live from the Nasdaq balcony while cameras flashed around him. Employees celebrated wildly. Early investors became multimillionaires overnight. Journalists surrounded Marcus asking questions about private jets, billionaire lifestyles, and the future of transportation.

For a brief moment, the excitement felt unstoppable.

But the reality inside the company looked very different.

The technology still required years of refinement. Manufacturing costs remained extremely high. Commercial adoption was slower than expected. Competitors introduced new products aggressively. Regulatory approvals created constant delays.

Yet public investors expected immediate growth.

Every quarterly earnings report became a battle. Analysts demanded faster deployment numbers. Investors questioned profitability timelines. Short sellers criticized the company's projections publicly. Social media traders treated the stock like a casino.

Marcus felt trapped between operational reality and investor expectations.

One evening, after a brutal earnings call triggered a twenty-five percent stock decline, Marcus sat alone inside QuantumDrive's headquarters reviewing online investor comments.

"Overhyped SPAC scam."

"Fake projections."

"Another billionaire founder cashing out."

The words hit harder than he expected.

He had never intended to mislead anyone. He genuinely believed in the company's technology. But somewhere along the way, the public narrative surrounding QuantumDrive had grown larger than the business itself.

The following month, rising interest rates triggered a collapse across growth stocks.

Companies that once traded at massive valuations suddenly lost seventy or eighty percent of their value. Investors abandoned speculative technology plays rapidly.

QuantumDrive's stock crashed.

Within eight months, the company's valuation fell from nearly $9 billion to under $1.5 billion.

Employees panicked as stock options became nearly worthless. Layoff rumors spread internally. Financial media outlets that once celebrated Marcus now questioned whether SPAC-era companies had become symbols of market excess.

Board meetings grew increasingly tense.

"We need immediate cost reductions," said the CFO during one emergency meeting.

"We cut too deeply and we lose engineering progress," Marcus argued.

“We don’t have a choice anymore,” another board member replied bluntly.

For the first time since founding the company, Marcus began questioning whether going public so early had been a mistake.

The pressure became relentless.

Every public appearance triggered criticism. Investors accused management of overpromising. Journalists highlighted declining stock performance constantly. Online traders mocked former SPAC companies daily.

One night, Marcus drove alone into the Arizona desert outside Phoenix.

He parked near an abandoned highway construction site and stared across the empty landscape beneath the stars.

Years earlier, he imagined building revolutionary technology that would change transportation forever. He never imagined becoming trapped inside a financial spectacle driven by speculation, momentum trading, and impossible expectations.

His phone rang.

It was Elena Ruiz, QuantumDrive’s head engineer.

“You disappeared,” she said.

"I needed to think."

There was silence for a moment.

"Do you still believe in the technology?" she asked quietly.

Marcus looked toward the horizon.

"Yes."

"Then stop focusing on the stock price."

Her words stayed with him.

Over the following year, Marcus radically changed his approach.

Thc company abandoned aggressive public projections. Marketing budgets were reduced. Expansion slowed. Management focused entirely on improving operational efficiency, product reliability, and commercial partnerships.

The transition was painful.

The stock remained volatile. Media attention faded. Several early investors exited completely.

But slowly, the business itself improved.

Autonomous freight contracts expanded steadily. Logistics companies began adopting the technology more broadly. Revenue growth stabilized based on actual deployment rather than speculative forecasts.

Three years later, QuantumDrive was no longer viewed as a hype-driven SPAC sensation.

It had become a real operating business. The valuation never returned to its peak speculative levels, but the company survived while many other SPAC-era businesses collapsed entirely.

During an entrepreneurship conference years later, a young founder approached Marcus after his speech.

“Would you do the SPAC again?” the founder asked.

Marcus smiled thoughtfully.

“The capital helped us survive,” he admitted. “But the hype almost destroyed us.”

The founder looked confused.

“What do you mean?”

Marcus leaned back in his chair before answering.

"There's a difference between building a valuable company and building a valuable stock story. Public markets eventually figure out which one you actually created."

Chapter 4

Reverse Mergers and Other Alternative Paths to Public Markets

The financial markets have always evolved alongside entrepreneurship, technology, and investor demand. While traditional initial public offerings remain one of the most recognized methods for companies to become publicly traded, they are far from the only path available. Over time, businesses, investors, and financial professionals have developed alternative strategies that allow companies to access public capital markets through less conventional structures. Among these methods, reverse mergers have played one of the most important and controversial roles in shaping alternative public offerings.

A reverse merger, sometimes called a reverse takeover or reverse IPO, occurs when a private company merges with an existing publicly traded company, often one with minimal active operations. Through this transaction, the private company effectively gains public market status without completing a traditional IPO process. While the concept may initially sound unusual, reverse mergers have existed for decades and have served as an important financial shortcut for companies seeking faster or less expensive access to public markets.

To understand why reverse mergers became popular, it is important to first examine the limitations of traditional IPOs. Conventional IPOs involve lengthy preparation timelines, underwriting negotiations, regulatory reviews, financial audits, investor roadshows, and substantial costs. For smaller companies or businesses operating in emerging industries, the process can become prohibitively expensive or strategically inefficient. Some companies may lack the size or profitability levels traditionally favored by major institutional investors and investment banks. Others may need capital more urgently than the traditional IPO timeline allows.

Reverse mergers emerged as a solution to some of these challenges. Instead of building an IPO from the ground up, a private company essentially takes control of an already-public entity. In many cases, the public company involved in the transaction is a shell company—a corporation that maintains public registration but has little or no active business operations. By merging into this shell, the private company inherits the public listing and begins trading publicly.

The mechanics of a reverse merger are relatively straightforward in principle, although the actual legal and financial processes can be highly complex. The shareholders of the private company exchange their ownership interests for a controlling stake in the public shell company. After the merger closes, the management team of the private company usually assumes operational control of the newly combined entity. The private company's business operations effectively become the primary operations of the public company.

One of the greatest advantages of reverse mergers is speed. Traditional IPOs can take many months or years to complete, while reverse mergers may sometimes close much more quickly. This speed can be highly valuable for companies operating in rapidly evolving industries where access to capital and market visibility may determine competitive survival. Companies needing immediate funding for expansion, acquisitions, manufacturing, or research may prefer alternative public offering structures that reduce delays.

Cost savings also represent a significant advantage. Traditional IPOs often involve substantial underwriting fees, legal expenses, accounting costs, marketing expenditures, and compliance requirements. Reverse mergers can reduce some of these costs because the public entity already exists. Smaller companies that may not attract large underwriting syndicates often view reverse mergers as a more financially accessible route into public markets. Another major advantage involves reduced dependence on market timing. Traditional IPOs are highly sensitive to market conditions. A sudden economic downturn, geopolitical crisis, interest rate increase, or stock market correction can delay or derail an IPO entirely. Reverse mergers may offer greater flexibility because they are negotiated privately rather than relying entirely on institutional investor demand during a specific offering window.

For founders and early investors, reverse mergers may also provide faster liquidity opportunities. Once the company becomes publicly traded, shares may eventually become tradable on public exchanges or over-the-counter markets. This can create exit opportunities for early shareholders who have spent years building the business privately.

Throughout financial history, many companies have used reverse mergers successfully to access public markets. Some eventually grew into substantial businesses with strong revenues, loyal customer bases, and long-term shareholder value creation. Others, however, became examples of the risks associated with weak oversight, poor governance, or speculative market behavior.

One major concern surrounding reverse mergers involves due diligence and regulatory scrutiny. Traditional IPOs typically involve extensive review by investment banks, institutional investors, auditors, attorneys, and regulators. Reverse mergers may sometimes involve less rigorous vetting processes, increasing the risk that weaker companies enter public markets without sufficient operational maturity or financial stability.

This issue became particularly visible during periods when large numbers of speculative companies used reverse mergers to access public markets rapidly. Some businesses entering through reverse mergers lacked strong internal controls, reliable financial reporting systems, or sustainable business models. In certain cases, fraudulent companies exploited reverse merger structures to create the appearance of legitimacy while misleading investors.

As a result, regulators and exchanges increased scrutiny of reverse merger transactions over time. Stock exchanges implemented stricter listing standards, while regulatory agencies introduced additional reporting and compliance requirements designed to protect investors and improve transparency. These changes aimed to separate legitimate growth companies from speculative or poorly managed businesses.

Another important risk associated with reverse mergers involves reputation and market perception. Some institutional investors view reverse mergers less favorably than traditional IPOs because they may perceive them as lower-quality public offerings. Companies entering public markets through reverse mergers sometimes face skepticism regarding their financial strength, governance standards, or long-term viability. Overcoming these perceptions often requires strong operational performance and transparent communication with investors.

Liquidity can also become a challenge. Newly public companies resulting from reverse mergers may initially trade with lower volume and reduced institutional participation compared to traditional IPOs. Limited liquidity can increase stock price volatility and make it more difficult for investors to enter or exit positions efficiently. Building investor confidence often takes time and consistent business execution.

Despite these risks, reverse mergers continue to represent an important financial tool because they offer flexibility and accessibility within the broader capital market ecosystem. Not every company fits the traditional IPO model. Some businesses may benefit from alternative pathways that align more effectively with their size, timing needs, strategic goals, or industry conditions.

Reverse mergers are only one category of alternative public offerings. Another increasingly important method involves direct listings. In a direct listing, a private company becomes publicly traded without issuing new shares or relying heavily on traditional underwriters. Existing shareholders sell shares directly into the public market. This structure can reduce underwriting costs and minimize dilution because the company is not necessarily raising new capital during the listing process.

Direct listings became especially attractive for companies with strong brand recognition, significant cash reserves, and substantial existing investor interest. Technology companies with loyal customer bases and large private valuations sometimes viewed direct listings as more efficient alternatives to traditional IPOs. By avoiding heavy underwriting involvement, companies gained greater control over pricing and reduced certain transaction costs.

However, direct listings also present challenges. Because no new shares are typically issued initially, companies may not raise additional operating capital through the listing itself. In addition, without underwriters stabilizing the market, stock prices may experience significant volatility during initial trading periods.

Another important category of alternative public offerings involves over-the-counter markets, commonly known as OTC markets. Smaller companies sometimes begin trading publicly through OTC exchanges before eventually seeking listings on larger national exchanges such as Nasdaq or the New York Stock Exchange. OTC markets provide access to public trading while often involving less stringent listing requirements than major exchanges.

For smaller or early-stage businesses, OTC markets may serve as stepping stones toward larger public market opportunities. However, OTC companies often face challenges involving liquidity, investor confidence, transparency, and regulatory perception. Investors must carefully evaluate financial disclosures and operational quality when analyzing smaller public companies.

The evolution of alternative public offerings reflects broader changes in entrepreneurship and global finance. Modern startups scale faster than ever before. Technology enables businesses to reach global markets rapidly. Investors seek earlier access to growth opportunities. Public participation in financial markets has expanded dramatically through online trading platforms and digital investing communities. These trends create demand for more flexible and diverse capital-raising structures.

Alternative public offerings also highlight the growing importance of narrative and perception within modern markets. Investors increasingly focus not only on historical financial performance but also on future growth potential, scalability, industry disruption, and innovation. Companies capable of presenting compelling long-term visions may attract substantial investor attention even before achieving consistent profitability.

At the same time, the rise of alternative public offerings demonstrates the dangers of speculation and hype. During periods of excessive market optimism, investors may become overly focused on narratives while ignoring operational realities. Companies with weak fundamentals can temporarily achieve inflated valuations driven more by momentum than sustainable business performance. Eventually, however, public markets tend to reward companies capable of delivering real execution and punish those that fail to meet expectations.

For founders, choosing the right path to public markets requires strategic thinking. A traditional IPO may offer prestige and institutional credibility. A SPAC may provide speed and valuation certainty. A reverse merger may offer cost efficiency and faster execution. A direct listing may reduce dilution. Each method carries unique trade-offs involving cost, control, liquidity, regulatory complexity, and long-term shareholder dynamics. Understanding these alternatives is increasingly important because capital markets will likely continue evolving. Financial innovation rarely remains static. New technologies such as blockchain systems, tokenized securities, decentralized finance platforms, and digital assets may eventually create entirely new methods for companies to raise capital and achieve liquidity. Future public market structures may look dramatically different from those used today.

One of the most important lessons within alternative public offerings is that becoming public does not guarantee long-term success. Public market access simply creates opportunity. Sustained wealth creation still depends on operational execution, financial discipline, leadership quality, customer demand, strategic adaptability, and investor trust. Companies that fail to build sustainable businesses eventually struggle regardless of how they initially entered the public markets.

Investors must similarly remain disciplined when evaluating alternative public offerings. Exciting narratives and innovative industries can create substantial opportunities, but they can also produce excessive speculation and volatility. Understanding the mechanics, incentives, and risks behind each structure allows investors to make more informed decisions and avoid blindly following market hype.

Alternative public offerings ultimately represent an important part of the broader financial ecosystem because they expand access to capital markets and create strategic flexibility for businesses. While traditional IPOs remain highly valuable, they are no longer the only route toward public company status. Entrepreneurs today operate in a financial world filled with multiple pathways to growth, liquidity, and long-term wealth creation.

As markets continue evolving, founders and investors who understand these alternative structures will possess valuable advantages. They will be better prepared to recognize opportunities, evaluate risks intelligently, and navigate the increasingly complex world of modern capital markets. Reverse mergers, direct listings, SPACs, and future innovations all reflect a deeper truth about entrepreneurship and finance: markets constantly adapt to changing economic realities, investor behavior, and technological progress.

The Forgotten Shell Company

David Mercer leaned back in his chair as the rain hammered against the windows of his small office in downtown Seattle. It was nearly midnight, and the glow from his computer monitor illuminated stacks of financial reports covering the desk.

For the third time that week, another venture capital firm had rejected his company.

After five years building HelioWave Medical Technologies, David was running out of time.

The company specialized in advanced wearable medical monitoring devices capable of detecting early cardiac abnormalities using artificial intelligence. Doctors loved the technology. Patients participating in trials showed promising results. But manufacturing expansion required millions of dollars the company no longer possessed.

Payroll deadlines approached quickly.

Competitors with larger funding rounds were entering the market aggressively.

Traditional financing options were disappearing.

"We can survive maybe six more months," said Claire Donovan, the company's CFO, during an emergency board meeting the next morning.

The room fell silent.

David stared at the whiteboard projections showing rapidly declining cash reserves. Years earlier, he believed groundbreaking technology alone would guarantee investor support. Now he understood that survival depended as much on capital access as innovation itself.

"What about an IPO?" one board member asked.

Claire shook her head immediately.

"We're too small for a traditional IPO. Revenue isn't large enough, and the process would take too long anyway."

The discussion continued for hours without solutions.

Then an older board member named Richard Lawson spoke quietly from the corner of the room.

"There may be another option."

Everyone turned toward him.

"A reverse merger."

David frowned. "With a shell company?"

Richard nodded slowly.

"I know a group that controls an old publicly traded corporation with almost no active operations left. The company still maintains SEC registration."

Claire looked skeptical. “That market has a terrible reputation.”

“Some deals do,” Richard admitted. “But not all.” Three weeks later, David sat inside a law office conference room in Los Angeles reviewing documents for a company called Meridian Global Holdings.

The corporation once operated a chain of industrial supply businesses decades earlier before collapsing financially. Now it existed primarily as a dormant public shell trading lightly on over-the-counter markets.

Its remaining assets consisted mostly of public registration status.

“This gives you immediate public market access,” explained the attorney leading the transaction discussions.

David studied the paperwork carefully.

“So HelioWave shareholders would take control of the public entity?”

“Correct.”

“And we avoid the traditional IPO process?”

The attorney nodded.

"It's significantly faster and less expensive."

Despite lingering doubts, David recognized the opportunity.

Within four months, the reverse merger closed.

HelioWave Medical Technologies officially became publicly traded under the ticker HMWT.

For the first time in the company's history, public investors could purchase shares directly.

The initial reaction was modest.

Unlike massive IPOs or SPAC mergers dominating financial headlines, HelioWave received little mainstream attention. Trading volume remained low. Institutional investors largely ignored the company.

But the public listing created something critically important: credibility.

Suddenly, suppliers took the company more seriously. Potential partners became more responsive. Smaller institutional investors began scheduling meetings. Additional financing opportunities emerged gradually.

Still, public life proved challenging.

The company now faced SEC reporting requirements, quarterly disclosures, governance obligations, and increased legal expenses. Managing public compliance consumed enormous amounts of time and resources.

Then came the online critics.

Financial message boards mocked small OTC-listed companies relentlessly.

“Another reverse merger scam.”

“Worthless penny stock.”

“Fake medical tech hype.”

David tried ignoring the comments, but the negativity frustrated him deeply.

HelioWave’s technology was real. Doctors genuinely supported the products. Patients benefited from early detection systems.

Yet public market perception often ignored operational reality.

One evening, David attended a small investor conference in Chicago hoping to attract institutional interest. Most attendees crowded around larger technology companies while HelioWave’s presentation room remained nearly empty.

After the session ended, an older investor approached quietly.

"I've seen hundreds of companies like yours," the investor said.

David sighed tiredly. "And?"

"Most fail."

David nodded.

"I know." The investor studied him carefully.

"But the few that survive usually focus less on stock promotion and more on execution."

Those words stayed with David.

Over the next two years, HelioWave operated with relentless discipline.

Instead of chasing media hype, management focused on product reliability, regulatory approvals, hospital partnerships, and manufacturing efficiency. Growth remained slower than investors initially hoped, but the business steadily improved operationally.

Gradually, revenue increased.

Then profitability emerged.

Several regional hospital networks signed long-term contracts. Insurance companies began supporting reimbursement programs. Medical journals published positive research regarding the company's monitoring systems.

Institutional investors slowly started paying attention.

By the company's fourth year as a public entity, HelioWave qualified for uplisting to Nasdaq.

The announcement transformed investor perception almost overnight.

Financial media outlets that once ignored the company suddenly described it as an emerging medical technology success story. Trading volume surged. Larger institutional funds initiated positions. Analysts published coverage reports praising management discipline and long-term growth potential.

David stood silently on the Nasdaq balcony during the uplisting ceremony watching the opening bell ring.

The moment felt surreal.

Years earlier, the company nearly collapsed from lack of funding. Now HelioWave operated internationally with growing revenues and expanding market recognition.

After the ceremony, a young entrepreneur approached David nervously.

"I heard your company started through a reverse merger," he said.

David smiled slightly.

"We did."

"Would you recommend it?" David paused thoughtfully before answering.

"A reverse merger doesn't build the business for you," he said. "It only opens the door."

The entrepreneur looked curious.

"So what matters most?"

David glanced across the trading floor below.

"What you do after you walk through it."

The evolution of public markets has accelerated dramatically over the past several decades. Technological innovation, globalization, online investing platforms, social media, and changing investor behavior have reshaped how companies raise capital and how investors participate in wealth creation opportunities. While traditional initial public offerings once dominated the public listing landscape almost entirely, alternative methods such as SPACs, reverse mergers, and direct listings have emerged as important components of modern capital markets. Among these alternatives, direct listings represent one of the most fascinating developments because they challenge many long-standing assumptions about how companies should enter the public markets.

Direct listings gained prominence as successful technology companies began questioning whether the traditional IPO system fully aligned with their interests. Founders, executives, and early investors increasingly argued that conventional IPOs often involved excessive underwriting fees, unnecessary dilution, restricted market pricing mechanisms, and disproportionate influence from large institutional investors.

Chapter 5

Direct Listings and the Future of Public Market Access

The evolution of public markets has accelerated dramatically over the last several decades. Technological innovation, globalization, digital investing platforms, social media, and changing investor behavior have reshaped how companies raise capital and how investors participate in wealth creation opportunities. While traditional initial public offerings once dominated the public listing landscape almost exclusively, alternative methods such as SPACs, reverse mergers, and direct listings have emerged as important components of modern capital markets. Among these alternatives, direct listings represent one of the most fascinating developments because they challenge many long-standing assumptions about how companies should enter the public markets.

Direct listings gained prominence as successful technology companies began questioning whether the traditional IPO system fully aligned with their interests. Founders, executives, and early investors increasingly argued that conventional IPOs often involved excessive underwriting fees, unnecessary dilution, restricted market pricing mechanisms, and disproportionate influence from large institutional investors.

Direct listings emerged as an alternative approach designed to provide companies with greater flexibility, transparency, and market-driven price discovery.

To understand the significance of direct listings, it is important to first understand how traditional IPOs normally function. In a traditional IPO, investment banks underwrite the offering by helping the company prepare financial filings, market the shares to institutional investors, determine pricing, and stabilize the stock during the initial trading period. The company issues new shares to raise capital, and underwriters receive substantial fees for managing the process. Institutional investors often receive priority access to shares before public trading begins.

This system has existed for decades and has successfully helped countless companies access public markets. However, critics argue that the traditional IPO structure sometimes disadvantages founders and existing shareholders. In some cases, IPO shares are priced conservatively to ensure strong initial trading performance, leading to dramatic first-day stock surges that suggest the company may have sold shares too cheaply. While institutional investors benefiting from early allocations may profit significantly, the issuing company may effectively leave billions of dollars on the table. Direct listings attempt to address some of these concerns by removing certain traditional underwriting elements from the process. In a direct listing, a company becomes publicly traded without issuing large amounts of new shares through a traditional underwritten offering. Instead, existing shareholders such as founders, employees, venture capital firms, and early investors sell their shares directly into the public market once trading begins.

This approach fundamentally changes how the listing process operates. Rather than relying heavily on underwriters to set pricing, the market itself determines the opening share price through supply and demand. Existing shareholders gain greater flexibility regarding liquidity, while companies may reduce underwriting fees and avoid some forms of dilution associated with issuing new shares.

One reason direct listings became attractive for large technology companies was because many of these businesses already possessed substantial cash reserves before going public. Unlike earlier generations of companies that primarily pursued IPOs to raise critical operating capital, some modern technology firms had already secured billions of dollars through private funding rounds. Their primary objective in becoming public was not necessarily raising new money but rather creating liquidity for employees and investors while expanding market visibility. Companies pursuing direct listings often believe that market-driven pricing creates fairer valuations. Instead of relying heavily on institutional book-building processes controlled by underwriters, opening prices emerge more organically based on investor demand. Supporters argue this creates greater transparency and reduces the likelihood of severe underpricing during initial trading.

Another major advantage of direct listings involves reduced lockup restrictions. In traditional IPOs, insiders are often prohibited from selling shares for a specified period following the offering. Direct listings may provide greater flexibility for existing shareholders seeking liquidity. Employees holding stock options or early investors who supported the company privately for many years may appreciate the ability to access public markets more immediately.

Direct listings can also reduce certain conflicts of interest associated with traditional underwriting relationships. In some IPOs, critics argue that underwriters may prioritize relationships with large institutional clients who receive favorable share allocations. Direct listings shift more responsibility toward open market pricing mechanisms rather than negotiated institutional allocations.

However, direct listings also introduce significant challenges and risks. One of the most important concerns involves volatility. Traditional underwriters often play stabilizing roles during IPO trading by supporting liquidity and managing investor demand. Without these mechanisms, direct listings may experience larger price swings during initial trading periods. Market sentiment, investor psychology, and trading momentum can significantly impact opening valuations.

Another challenge involves capital raising limitations. Because direct listings historically focused on allowing existing shareholders to sell shares rather than issuing large amounts of new equity, companies may not immediately raise substantial operating capital through the process itself. Businesses requiring significant expansion funding may still prefer traditional IPOs or alternative structures capable of generating large cash inflows.

Investor education also becomes critically important in direct listings. Without extensive underwriting roadshows and institutional marketing campaigns, companies must communicate their business models, growth strategies, and financial positions effectively to public investors. Transparency and investor confidence remain essential for successful trading performance.

The rise of direct listings reflects broader shifts occurring throughout modern financial markets. Technology has democratized investing access dramatically. Millions of retail investors now participate directly in stock markets through online brokerages and mobile trading platforms. Information spreads globally within seconds through financial media, social networks, online forums, podcasts, and digital communities. Investors increasingly seek direct participation in growth opportunities that were once primarily available to institutional players.

This democratization of investing has transformed how companies think about public offerings. Modern businesses often possess strong brand recognition and direct customer relationships long before entering public markets. Social media engagement, online communities, and digital ecosystems allow companies to build investor awareness organically. Some businesses no longer view traditional underwriting structures as the only effective path toward public market participation.

At the same time, the rise of direct listings also highlights changing attitudes toward corporate ownership and liquidity. In earlier decades, private companies often remained relatively inaccessible to ordinary investors until formal IPOs occurred. Today, massive private funding rounds allow startups to achieve multibillion-dollar valuations before ever entering public markets. By the time traditional IPOs occur, much of the early-stage growth may already belong to private institutional investors. Direct listings may help address this imbalance by creating broader market participation earlier in the public trading lifecycle. Supporters argue that reducing artificial pricing mechanisms and institutional allocation advantages creates fairer market access for ordinary investors.

However, direct listings do not eliminate the fundamental realities of investing risk. Companies entering public markets through direct listings remain subject to the same operational challenges, economic cycles, competitive pressures, and investor expectations as traditionally listed businesses. Public market success still depends primarily on execution, profitability, scalability, governance, and long-term strategic discipline.

The evolution of direct listings also intersects with broader discussions about the future of capital markets themselves. Financial innovation continues accelerating rapidly. Blockchain technology, tokenized assets, decentralized finance systems, digital securities, and artificial intelligence-driven trading platforms may fundamentally reshape how companies raise capital and distribute ownership in the future.

Some financial experts believe future public offerings may eventually operate through highly decentralized digital marketplaces where investors participate globally without relying heavily on traditional intermediaries. Smart contracts, blockchain verification systems, and tokenized ownership structures could potentially reduce transaction costs, increase transparency, and create continuous liquidity across global markets.

While these developments remain speculative, the rise of direct listings demonstrates that long-standing financial systems are increasingly open to disruption and experimentation. Capital markets evolve continuously in response to technology, investor behavior, regulation, and economic incentives. Companies and investors capable of adapting to these changes may gain substantial strategic advantages.

Another important lesson from direct listings involves founder control and corporate governance. Many technology founders seek structures allowing them to maintain long-term strategic control even after becoming public. Dual-class share systems, voting control arrangements, and alternative governance structures have become increasingly common among innovative companies seeking to balance public ownership with founder-led vision.

This reflects a broader philosophical shift within entrepreneurship. Many modern founders prioritize long-term innovation over short-term quarterly performance pressures. They seek public market access while preserving strategic flexibility and operational independence. Direct listings sometimes align more naturally with these objectives because they may involve less dilution and fewer institutional constraints during the transition into public markets.

Nevertheless, direct listings are not appropriate for every company. Businesses lacking strong brand recognition, stable financial performance, or substantial investor interest may struggle without the support structures provided by traditional underwriters. Smaller or less established companies may still benefit significantly from conventional IPO marketing, institutional investor relationships, and capital-raising capabilities.

Choosing between traditional IPOs, SPACs, reverse mergers, direct listings, or future alternative structures ultimately depends on a company's specific objectives, financial position, growth strategy, and market environment. No single structure guarantees success. Each method involves trade-offs related to cost, control, liquidity, volatility, investor access, governance, and long-term strategic positioning.

For investors, understanding direct listings requires analyzing both business fundamentals and broader market dynamics. Public excitement surrounding innovative listing structures should never replace disciplined evaluation of financial statements, competitive positioning, leadership quality, scalability, and operational execution. Exciting narratives alone cannot sustain long-term shareholder value without underlying business strength.

The future of public market access will likely involve continued diversification and experimentation. Traditional IPOs will remain important, but alternative structures will continue evolving as technology and investor behavior change. Companies may increasingly customize listing strategies based on unique operational needs and market opportunities.

Ultimately, direct listings symbolize a broader transformation occurring throughout modern finance. Markets are becoming more digital, decentralized, transparent, and globally interconnected. Investors possess greater access to information and participation opportunities than at any point in history. Companies possess more flexibility regarding how they raise capital and structure ownership.

For entrepreneurs, investors, and financial professionals, understanding these changes is essential. The future of wealth creation will likely involve navigating increasingly sophisticated and rapidly evolving capital market systems. Those capable of understanding these shifts intelligently may position themselves advantageously within the next generation of global finance and public market innovation.

The Day the Market Chose the Price

Aiden Brooks stood quietly inside the glass-walled conference room overlooking San Francisco Bay as dawn slowly illuminated the city skyline. Ferries crossed the water beneath layers of gray morning fog while inside the office, dozens of employees stared nervously at computer monitors displaying pre-market trading data.

Today, his company would become public.

But unlike most companies entering Wall Street, there would be no traditional IPO roadshow, no ceremonial underwriter pricing process, and no massive institutional allocation agreements controlling the opening valuation.

Today, the market itself would decide what his company was worth.

Nimbus Social Technologies had become one of the fastest-growing communication platforms in the world. What started as a small messaging app built in Aiden's apartment had evolved into a global social networking ecosystem used by over four hundred million people.

The company generated billions in annual revenue.

It also possessed billions in private cash reserves after years of venture capital investment.

Which was exactly why Aiden rejected the traditional IPO process.

"We don't need Wall Street to tell us our value," he had told his board months earlier.

Instead, Nimbus chose a direct listing.

The decision shocked much of the financial industry.

Major investment banks aggressively pushed for a traditional IPO, promising massive institutional demand and extensive underwriting support. Analysts estimated the banks could earn hundreds of millions in fees managing the offering.

But Aiden disliked the entire system.

He hated the idea of underwriters deciding which institutional investors received preferential access to shares before ordinary investors could participate. He disliked the massive first-day price spikes that often enriched hedge funds while companies themselves received no additional benefit.

Most importantly, Nimbus did not need additional capital.

The company already had enough money to operate independently for years.

What Aiden wanted was liquidity for employees and investors while allowing open-market pricing to determine the company's valuation naturally.

Still, the risks terrified him.

Without underwriters stabilizing the stock, volatility could become extreme.

Critics warned the stock might collapse immediately.

Others feared chaos without institutional pricing control mechanisms.

Financial media debated the direct listing endlessly for weeks leading up to launch day.

"This could reshape the future of public offerings," one analyst argued on television.

"Or become a disaster," another replied.

Inside Nimbus headquarters, employees watched nervously as opening market orders accumulated rapidly.

Claire Monroe, the company's CFO, approached Aiden holding updated market data. "Demand looks strong," she said cautiously.

"How strong?"

She exhaled slowly.

"Potentially much stronger than anyone expected."

At 9:30 a.m., Nasdaq officially opened trading.

For several tense minutes, Nimbus shares remained halted while market makers attempted to balance buy and sell orders. Millions of investors worldwide watched the screens waiting for the opening price.

Then suddenly the ticker activated.

NMBX opened nearly sixty percent above the company's last private valuation.

Cheers erupted throughout Nimbus headquarters.

Employees hugged each other. Early engineers who once accepted tiny salaries in exchange for stock options stared in disbelief at their account balances. Financial reporters flooded social media with reactions as trading volume exploded globally.

By midday, Nimbus briefly surpassed a $70 billion valuation.

Aiden appeared on financial television later that afternoon.

"Do you think this proves direct listings are the future?" the interviewer asked excitedly.

Aiden smiled carefully.

"I think it proves markets are evolving."

But privately, he knew the real challenge had only begun.

Over the following months, Nimbus experienced intense volatility.

Without traditional lockup restrictions, some early investors sold aggressively. Retail traders treated the stock like a momentum trade. Social media speculation amplified every news headline.

Quarterly earnings reports became global media events.

Analysts questioned user growth rates, advertising revenue trends, artificial intelligence investments, and international expansion costs constantly.

Aiden quickly realized public markets demanded endless performance. One evening after a brutal earnings selloff erased nearly $12 billion in market value within hours, Aiden sat alone inside the dark office staring across the city.

The stock chart glowing on his monitor looked violent and unpredictable.

His phone buzzed repeatedly with media requests, investor concerns, and analyst commentary.

For the first time since founding Nimbus, he questioned whether becoming public had been worth it.

Then came the recession.

Advertising markets weakened sharply. Technology valuations collapsed across the sector. Investors abandoned growth companies rapidly in favor of safer assets.

Nimbus shares fell more than fifty percent.

Financial journalists suddenly criticized companies that once symbolized innovation and digital transformation. Retail investors who purchased shares near the peak accused management of overvaluation and unrealistic expectations.

Inside the company, employee morale declined sharply as stock compensation lost value.

Board meetings grew tense.

"We need stronger profitability metrics," one board member insisted. "If we cut innovation spending now, we risk long-term competitiveness," Aiden argued.

"But Wall Street wants earnings."

Aiden leaned back silently.

That single sentence captured everything he disliked about public markets.

Yet despite the pressure, Nimbus remained operationally strong. User engagement continued growing globally. The company's cash reserves remained enormous. Core technology infrastructure improved steadily.

Aiden made a decision.

Instead of obsessing over short-term stock movements, Nimbus would focus entirely on long-term product development, artificial intelligence integration, and global expansion.

The next three years tested investors' patience severely.

But eventually, the strategy worked.

Nimbus launched new AI-driven communication systems that transformed digital collaboration globally. Enterprise clients expanded rapidly. Revenue diversified beyond advertising. Profitability improved substantially. Slowly, investor confidence returned.

By the company's fifth anniversary as a public entity, Nimbus had become one of the largest technology platforms in the world.

During a global entrepreneurship summit years later, a young founder asked Aiden what he learned from taking Nimbus public through a direct listing.

Aiden thought quietly before answering.

"Public markets are powerful," he said. "But they amplify everything."

The founder looked curious.

"What do you mean?"

"If your business is strong, public markets can accelerate growth and wealth creation," Aiden explained. "But if your business is weak, they expose every weakness faster than you can imagine."

The founder nodded slowly.

"So the listing structure isn't the most important part?"

Aiden smiled.

"No. The company itself is."

Chapter 6

How Market Cycles and Investor Psychology Shape Alternative Public Offerings

Financial markets are driven not only by numbers, financial statements, and economic data, but also by emotion, perception, confidence, fear, optimism, and human behavior. Understanding investor psychology and market cycles is essential for anyone seeking to navigate the world of public offerings, SPACs, reverse mergers, direct listings, or capital markets in general. Throughout history, some of the greatest fortunes have been created during periods of optimism and expansion, while some of the largest financial losses have occurred when fear and panic overtook the markets. Alternative public offerings are especially sensitive to these cycles because they often involve growth-oriented companies, emerging industries, and future-based valuations that depend heavily on investor expectations.

One of the most important truths about capital markets is that valuations are rarely based solely on current financial performance. Public markets constantly attempt to price future possibilities. Investors buy shares based on what they believe a company may become years into the future rather than only what it is today. This creates tremendous opportunity for innovative businesses, but it also introduces volatility because expectations can shift rapidly when market sentiment changes.

During periods of strong economic growth and investor optimism, markets often reward companies aggressively for future potential. Investors become more willing to tolerate risk, accept lower profitability, and support ambitious expansion plans. Capital becomes abundant. Interest rates may remain relatively low. Financial institutions become more aggressive in lending and investing. During these periods, alternative public offerings such as SPACs and direct listings often flourish because investors seek exposure to high-growth opportunities and disruptive industries.

Bull markets create environments where optimism expands quickly throughout the financial system. Rising stock prices reinforce investor confidence, attracting additional capital into the markets. Media coverage becomes increasingly positive. Success stories dominate headlines. Entrepreneurs become more ambitious. Venture capital funding increases. Retail investors enter the markets aggressively seeking rapid gains. Public enthusiasm for innovation intensifies. This optimism can create powerful momentum for companies entering the public markets through alternative structures. Investors may focus heavily on long-term narratives, industry disruption, technological transformation, and visionary leadership. Companies operating in sectors such as artificial intelligence, electric vehicles, biotechnology, renewable energy, space exploration, cryptocurrency, and financial technology often attract enormous investor attention during these cycles.

SPACs became one of the clearest examples of how market psychology influences financial structures. During periods of strong market enthusiasm, investors poured billions of dollars into SPACs because they believed they were gaining early access to the next generation of revolutionary companies. Sponsors launched hundreds of SPACs targeting industries associated with future growth and innovation. Retail investors enthusiastically participated in transactions involving companies that sometimes had limited revenues but enormous projected market opportunities.

In many cases, valuations increased dramatically based more on optimism and momentum than traditional financial metrics. Investors focused on future addressable markets, projected revenue growth, and disruptive potential rather than current profitability or operational stability. Some companies achieved multibillion-dollar valuations despite generating minimal revenue because investors believed future market dominance would justify the prices eventually. This phenomenon reflects a fundamental aspect of investor psychology known as narrative investing. Humans naturally respond to compelling stories. Investors often become emotionally attached to visions of technological transformation, economic disruption, and future wealth creation. A powerful narrative can temporarily outweigh financial caution, particularly during periods of widespread market optimism.

However, market cycles eventually shift.

No bull market lasts forever. Economic conditions change. Interest rates rise. Inflation increases. Geopolitical uncertainty emerges. Corporate earnings weaken. Investor confidence declines. As optimism fades, financial markets transition into more defensive environments where risk tolerance decreases substantially.

During bearish market conditions, investor psychology changes rapidly. The same companies once praised for aggressive growth strategies may suddenly face criticism for lacking profitability or financial discipline. Investors become more cautious and prioritize stability, cash flow, earnings consistency, and risk management. Valuations contract sharply, especially for speculative growth companies dependent on future projections. This shift in psychology can dramatically impact alternative public offerings. SPAC transactions that appeared highly attractive during bullish conditions may struggle when investor enthusiasm weakens. Redemption rates may increase sharply. PIPE investors may withdraw support. Stock prices may collapse after mergers close if investors lose confidence in growth projections or broader market conditions deteriorate.

The SPAC boom and subsequent decline illustrated how quickly investor sentiment can reverse. During peak market enthusiasm, nearly every industry narrative attracted capital. Electric vehicle startups, autonomous transportation companies, artificial intelligence platforms, renewable energy ventures, and futuristic technologies received extraordinary valuations. Investors feared missing out on the next major wealth creation opportunity.

Then market conditions changed.

Rising interest rates reduced investor appetite for speculative growth companies. Economic uncertainty increased. Several highly publicized SPAC companies failed to meet projections or deliver operational performance. Investor confidence deteriorated rapidly. Stock prices collapsed across the sector, and many companies that once symbolized financial innovation became examples of speculative excess. This cycle demonstrated one of the most important realities of financial markets: liquidity and investor confidence are deeply interconnected. During periods of abundant liquidity and optimism, investors aggressively seek higher returns and become more willing to accept risk. When liquidity tightens or uncertainty increases, investors rapidly move toward safer assets and more conservative strategies.

Alternative public offerings are especially vulnerable to these shifts because they often involve companies with evolving business models, emerging technologies, or uncertain profitability timelines. Investors supporting these businesses are frequently making long-term bets on future industry transformation rather than relying solely on established operational histories.

Another important psychological factor influencing alternative public offerings involves fear of missing out, commonly known as FOMO. During strong bull markets, investors often fear being excluded from transformative opportunities. Media headlines showcasing massive stock gains reinforce emotional decision-making. Social media amplifies success stories, speculation, and momentum trading. Retail investors may enter positions quickly without fully understanding valuation risks or operational realities. This behavior can create feedback loops where rising prices attract more buyers, which then push prices even higher. Momentum becomes self-reinforcing temporarily. However, once sentiment shifts negatively, the same psychological dynamics can reverse rapidly. Fear replaces greed. Investors rush to exit positions simultaneously. Selling pressure accelerates declines.

Public markets therefore function not only as economic systems but also as emotional systems reflecting collective human behavior. Understanding this psychological dimension is essential for founders, executives, and investors alike.

For founders considering alternative public offerings, timing becomes critically important. Entering public markets during periods of strong investor enthusiasm may create higher valuations, greater liquidity, and easier capital raising conditions. However, companies must avoid becoming overly dependent on speculative momentum. Public market access should ideally support sustainable long-term business growth rather than temporary excitement alone.

Founders must also recognize that public markets amplify scrutiny. During bullish periods, investors may overlook operational weaknesses temporarily if they believe future growth potential remains compelling. But once market sentiment shifts, those same weaknesses may become major concerns. Companies lacking strong fundamentals often struggle significantly when investor optimism fades. Investor psychology also influences employee behavior within public companies. Rapidly rising stock prices may create excitement, motivation, and optimism throughout organizations. Employees holding stock options may feel financially empowered and deeply committed to the company's mission. However, severe stock declines can damage morale, create retention challenges, and increase internal uncertainty.

Leadership becomes especially important during volatile market cycles. Founders and executives must maintain strategic discipline even when market sentiment fluctuates dramatically. Companies that survive difficult cycles often focus on operational execution, cash management, customer value, and long-term positioning rather than becoming distracted by short-term stock price movements.

Another important lesson from market cycles involves the distinction between valuation and value. Valuation refers to what investors are temporarily willing to pay for a company's shares. Value reflects the underlying strength, profitability, scalability, and long-term earning potential of the business itself. During speculative periods, valuations may rise far above underlying value. During fearful periods, valuations may fall below intrinsic business quality. Successful long-term investors understand this distinction clearly. They recognize that market psychology creates both opportunities and risks. Rather than blindly following emotional momentum, disciplined investors evaluate businesses based on sustainable fundamentals, competitive advantages, management quality, and long-term market positioning.

The rise of social media and digital investing platforms has accelerated market psychology dramatically. Information spreads globally within seconds. Online communities discuss investment opportunities constantly. Influencers, analysts, financial commentators, and retail traders shape narratives rapidly. This environment can increase volatility because sentiment shifts occur much faster than in previous decades.

Alternative public offerings increasingly operate within this highly interconnected digital financial ecosystem. Companies must manage investor relations, media narratives, online perception, and public communication carefully. Reputation, transparency, and credibility become critically important in maintaining long-term investor confidence.

At the same time, market cycles should not be viewed purely negatively. Volatility and corrections are natural components of healthy financial systems. Periods of excessive speculation often require eventual recalibration. Corrections help restore more realistic valuations and force companies to focus on operational discipline rather than hype alone. Many of the strongest companies in history survived severe market downturns before eventually creating enormous long-term wealth. Businesses capable of adapting during difficult cycles often emerge stronger because competition weakens, inefficiencies are eliminated, and management teams become more disciplined.

For entrepreneurs, understanding market cycles can improve strategic decision-making regarding fundraising, expansion timing, hiring, acquisitions, and public offerings. For investors, understanding psychology can reduce emotional decision-making and improve long-term investment discipline.

Alternative public offerings will likely continue evolving as financial markets change. New technologies, regulatory frameworks, digital assets, decentralized finance systems, and global investing platforms may create additional innovation in how companies access capital and liquidity. However, regardless of how financial structures evolve technologically, human psychology will likely remain one of the most powerful forces shaping market behavior.

Fear and greed have influenced markets for centuries. Optimism and panic will continue driving cycles of expansion and contraction. Understanding these psychological forces provides valuable insight into why markets behave the way they do and why certain financial trends emerge repeatedly across generations.

Ultimately, the companies and investors who succeed over the long term are often those capable of maintaining discipline while others become emotional. They understand that market cycles are temporary but business fundamentals matter permanently. They recognize that public markets reward sustainable execution over time, even if speculative enthusiasm temporarily distorts valuations.

Alternative public offerings represent powerful financial opportunities, but they exist within broader systems shaped by human emotion, economic conditions, and investor behavior. Understanding these cycles allows founders and investors to navigate the markets more intelligently, avoid emotional extremes, and position themselves more effectively for long-term wealth creation.

When the Market Turned Against Them

Tyler Monroe stood silently inside the trading floor observation room as red numbers flashed across every monitor in sight. Financial news anchors spoke rapidly about collapsing growth stocks, rising interest rates, and panic spreading throughout technology markets. Below him, traders moved frantically across the exchange floor while billions of dollars evaporated from market valuations around the world.

Six months earlier, Tyler was celebrated as one of the brightest young entrepreneurs in Silicon Valley.

Now investors called his company a disaster.

His startup, AeroSphere Mobility, specialized in autonomous urban air transportation systems—electric aircraft designed to transport passengers across crowded metropolitan areas. The vision captured global attention almost instantly. Investors described the company as the future of transportation.

During the peak of the SPAC boom, Titan Sky Acquisition Corp. approached Tyler with a merger proposal valuing AeroSphere at nearly $6 billion.

At first, the number felt unreal.

The company had not yet achieved commercial profitability. Full regulatory approvals remained years away. Manufacturing infrastructure still needed major expansion.

But investors did not seem to care.

The market was obsessed with futuristic technology. Every investor presentation generated overwhelming excitement. Financial media outlets compared AeroSphere to the early days of Tesla and SpaceX. Retail investors flooded online forums discussing how flying transportation networks would transform urban life.

The SPAC merger closed quickly.

On the first day of public trading, AeroSphere's valuation surged above $10 billion.

Tyler became a financial celebrity overnight.

Magazine covers described him as "The Future of Urban Mobility." Television interviews portrayed him as a visionary founder changing civilization itself. Social media followers increased into the millions.

Inside the company, employees celebrated wildly as stock options created instant paper wealth.

Everything felt unstoppable.

Then the economy changed.

Inflation surged unexpectedly across global markets. Central banks began raising interest rates aggressively. Investors suddenly became far less willing to support speculative growth companies with uncertain profitability. The same investors who once celebrated futuristic projections now demanded immediate financial discipline. AeroSphere's stock began falling rapidly.

At first, management believed the decline was temporary.

"It's just market volatility," Tyler reassured employees during an internal meeting.

But the declines continued.

Twenty percent.

Thirty percent.

Fifty percent.

Financial analysts who once praised the company suddenly criticized its cash burn, regulatory uncertainty, and commercialization timeline. Television commentators described SPAC-era companies as symbols of excessive speculation.

The mood surrounding AeroSphere transformed almost overnight.

Inside headquarters, anxiety spread quickly.

Employees who once checked soaring stock prices constantly now avoided discussing the market entirely. Recruiting became harder. Investors grew hostile during earnings calls. Journalists published articles questioning whether urban air mobility would ever become economically viable.

One evening after another brutal trading session, Tyler sat alone inside the company's rooftop lounge overlooking San Francisco.

Rain covered the city skyline while financial alerts continued appearing across his phone.

AeroSphere's stock had fallen another eighteen percent that day.

His CFO, Lauren Chen, walked onto the rooftop quietly.

"We need to cut spending," she said carefully.

Tyler stared across the city silently.

"If we slow development now, competitors catch us."

"If we don't cut spending, we may run out of capital entirely."

The pressure became relentless.

Board members demanded restructuring plans. Investors questioned management credibility. Online traders mocked AeroSphere constantly across social media.

Tyler began doubting himself.

Had the company gone public too early?

Had investors simply fallen in love with an exciting story instead of a real business?

For the first time since founding AeroSphere, he considered stepping down.

Then one morning, while reviewing operational reports, Tyler noticed something important.

Despite the collapsing stock price, the company's underlying engineering progress remained strong.

Flight systems continued improving.

Battery efficiency increased.

Commercial pilot programs expanded successfully.

The business itself had not failed.

The market's mood had changed.

That realization shifted his entire perspective.

Instead of obsessing over daily stock fluctuations, Tyler reorganized the company around long-term operational execution. Marketing budgets were reduced dramatically. Expansion slowed. Engineering priorities focused on commercial viability rather than investor excitement.

The transition was painful.

Layoffs became necessary. Media attention faded. Retail investor enthusiasm disappeared almost completely.

But over time, AeroSphere stabilized.

Three years later, urban transportation regulations evolved significantly. Several major cities approved commercial autonomous air mobility infrastructure. AeroSphere secured long-term contracts with logistics providers and municipal transportation networks.

Gradually, institutional investors returned.

Not because of hype.

Because the business itself finally proved sustainable.

During an investor conference years later, a young entrepreneur approached Tyler after his presentation.

"How did you survive the crash?" the founder asked.

Tyler smiled thoughtfully.

"We stopped building for market excitement," he replied. "What did you build for instead?"

Tyler looked toward the audience before answering.

"Reality."

The founder looked confused.

Tyler continued quietly.

"Bull markets can make almost any dream look valuable. But eventually, markets ask whether the business underneath the dream is actually strong enough to survive."

Chapter 7

Institutional Investors, PIPE Financing, and Capital Raising Strategy

Capital is the lifeblood of business expansion, innovation, acquisitions, market dominance, and long-term wealth creation. Regardless of how revolutionary a company's products, technology, or vision may be, sustained growth often depends on access to sufficient financial resources. In the world of public offerings and alternative market structures, institutional investors and private financing arrangements play critically important roles in determining whether companies succeed or struggle after entering the public markets. Among thesc financing mechanisms, PIPE financing became one of the defining features of the SPAC era and remains an essential concept for understanding modern capital formation strategies.

PIPE financing, which stands for Private Investment in Public Equity, refers to a transaction where institutional investors purchase shares directly from a publicly traded company through a private placement arrangement. In the context of SPACs and alternative public offerings, PIPE financing often provides additional capital that supports mergers, stabilizes investor confidence, and strengthens the balance sheet of the newly public company. While PIPE structures existed long before the rise of SPACs, they became especially important because many SPAC mergers depended heavily on institutional investor participation to succeed.

To understand why PIPE financing matters, it is important to first understand the broader role of institutional investors within financial markets. Institutional investors include hedge funds, mutual funds, pension funds, sovereign wealth funds, insurance companies, private equity firms, venture capital firms, family offices, university endowments, and asset management companies. These organizations collectively manage trillions of dollars globally and represent some of the most influential participants within the financial system.

Institutional investors play a powerful role because they possess large pools of capital, sophisticated analytical capabilities, extensive market experience, and significant influence over investor sentiment. When respected institutional investors support a company publicly, their involvement often increases market confidence. Retail investors, analysts, and financial media frequently interpret institutional participation as validation of a company's business model, growth potential, and leadership quality.

During the SPAC boom, PIPE financing became especially important because SPAC structures contained inherent uncertainties related to shareholder redemptions. SPAC investors generally had the right to redeem their shares for cash before mergers closed if they disagreed with the proposed transaction or simply preferred to exit the investment. High redemption rates could dramatically reduce the amount of capital available to the merged company, potentially weakening the financial viability of the deal itself.

PIPE financing helped address this issue by securing additional capital commitments from institutional investors before the merger closed. These investors agreed to purchase shares directly, often at predetermined prices, providing financial stability and increasing confidence that sufficient funding would remain available even if some SPAC shareholders redeemed their shares.

For founders and executives, securing PIPE investors often became one of the most critical stages of the entire SPAC process. A successful PIPE round could strengthen market credibility, improve liquidity, reduce financing uncertainty, and support long-term expansion plans. Conversely, failure to attract institutional support sometimes signaled deeper concerns regarding valuation, business quality, or operational execution. Institutional investors evaluating PIPE opportunities typically conduct extensive due diligence before committing capital. They analyze financial statements, management quality, competitive positioning, market opportunity, operational scalability, customer demand, governance structures, and valuation assumptions carefully. Unlike speculative retail investors driven primarily by momentum or media narratives, institutional investors often focus heavily on long-term risk-adjusted return potential.

This due diligence process can benefit companies because it imposes additional discipline and scrutiny. Businesses seeking institutional support must present realistic financial projections, credible operational strategies, and sustainable growth plans. Institutional investors often challenge assumptions aggressively and demand transparency regarding risks and execution challenges.

However, institutional investors also negotiate aggressively to protect their interests. PIPE investments frequently involve discounted share prices, favorable terms, warrants, convertible securities, or additional protections designed to reduce downside risk. While these terms may help secure necessary funding, they can also create dilution for existing shareholders and complicate long-term ownership structures.

Dilution became one of the most debated aspects of SPAC-era financing structures. Between sponsor promotes, warrants, PIPE investments, employee stock compensation, and additional financing rounds, ownership percentages could shift substantially after transactions closed. Founders and retail investors sometimes underestimated how significantly dilution could impact future shareholder value.

Understanding dilution is essential because ownership percentages directly influence long-term wealth creation. A company's valuation may increase dramatically after becoming public, but if ownership stakes shrink excessively due to financing structures, the economic benefits for existing shareholders may be less substantial than expected. Successful founders and investors therefore pay close attention not only to valuation growth but also to capital structure efficiency.

Institutional investors also influence public market psychology in powerful ways. When respected hedge funds, pension funds, or asset managers participate in PIPE rounds, financial markets often interpret this as a positive signal regarding the company's prospects. Media coverage frequently emphasizes institutional participation because it increases perceived legitimacy and confidence surrounding the transaction.

At the same time, institutional investors can create volatility if they later exit positions aggressively. Large funds possess substantial trading power, and their buying or selling activity can significantly impact stock prices. Companies heavily dependent on institutional support may experience sharp market movements when investor sentiment shifts.

Another important aspect of capital raising strategy involves balancing short-term financing needs with long-term strategic control. Entrepreneurs often face difficult decisions regarding how much ownership they are willing to surrender in exchange for capital. Excessive dilution may weaken founder influence, while insufficient capital may limit growth opportunities.

Some founders prioritize maintaining long-term control even if it slows expansion. Others pursue aggressive financing strategies designed to maximize market share rapidly, accepting greater dilution as the cost of scaling quickly. Neither approach is universally correct. The optimal strategy depends on industry dynamics, competitive pressures, market timing, operational needs, and founder objectives.

Technology companies operating in winner-take-all markets often prioritize rapid scaling because market leadership may generate enormous long-term advantages. In industries such as artificial intelligence, software platforms, social networks, biotechnology, and digital infrastructure, securing capital quickly can determine whether a company dominates globally or loses to faster-moving competitors. Alternative public offerings became especially attractive because they often accelerated access to institutional capital. Traditional private fundraising cycles could become time-consuming and restrictive. Public market access allowed companies to tap broader pools of investor capital while increasing liquidity and visibility simultaneously.

However, raising capital successfully requires more than simply presenting exciting narratives. Sophisticated institutional investors increasingly prioritize operational execution, governance quality, risk management, and financial discipline. The collapse of several highly publicized SPAC-era companies reinforced the importance of sustainable business fundamentals over speculative projections alone.

Institutional investors learned valuable lessons during the SPAC boom and subsequent market correction. During periods of extreme optimism, some investors supported transactions involving unrealistic growth assumptions or immature business models. As market conditions deteriorated, many funds became more selective and cautious regarding future investments.

This shift reflects a broader truth about financial markets: capital availability changes dramatically across economic cycles. During bullish environments characterized by low interest rates and abundant liquidity, investors often pursue aggressive growth opportunities more enthusiastically. During uncertain or bearish periods, investors become more defensive and prioritize profitability, cash flow, and operational resilience.

For companies seeking capital, understanding these cycles is critically important. Timing can influence valuations, financing costs, investor appetite, and negotiating leverage substantially. Businesses capable of raising capital during favorable market environments may gain strategic advantages that allow them to survive later downturns more effectively.

Another major component of capital raising strategy involves storytelling and communication. Investors do not simply evaluate financial statements mechanically. They evaluate visions of the future. Founders capable of communicating compelling narratives regarding market opportunities, technological disruption, scalability, and long-term value creation often attract stronger investor interest.

However, effective storytelling must remain grounded in operational reality. Overpromising and underdelivering can destroy investor confidence rapidly once public scrutiny intensifies. Sustainable credibility requires balancing optimism with transparency and disciplined execution.

Investor relations therefore become critically important after companies enter public markets. Public companies must communicate regularly with shareholders, analysts, institutions, and media outlets. Quarterly earnings calls, investor presentations, annual reports, and strategic updates shape market perception continuously.

Strong investor communication can help companies maintain confidence during difficult periods, while poor communication may amplify uncertainty and volatility. Founders who previously operated primarily within private startup environments often underestimate how demanding public market communication can become.

Another important consideration involves strategic partnerships. Institutional investors sometimes provide value beyond capital itself. Experienced investors may offer industry expertise, strategic relationships, operational guidance, acquisition opportunities, and credibility within financial markets. Choosing the right investors can therefore influence long-term business development significantly.

Sophisticated founders often evaluate investors carefully before accepting capital. Not all money creates equal strategic value. Some investors align more effectively with long-term company vision, while others prioritize shorter-term financial outcomes. Misalignment between management and investors can create significant operational tension after public offerings.

The future of capital raising will likely continue evolving as financial technology advances. Artificial intelligence, blockchain systems, decentralized finance platforms, tokenized assets, and global digital investment networks may eventually reshape how institutional and retail investors participate in capital markets. Companies may gain access to increasingly diverse financing structures that reduce reliance on traditional intermediaries.

Nevertheless, regardless of technological innovation, one principle will likely remain constant: capital flows toward opportunity, confidence, and execution. Investors ultimately seek businesses capable of generating sustainable value over time. Public market structures may evolve, but operational fundamentals and strategic leadership will remain essential drivers of long-term wealth creation.

Institutional investors and PIPE financing therefore represent far more than technical financial concepts. They symbolize the deeper relationship between capital, trust, growth, and market confidence within the modern economy. Understanding these dynamics provides entrepreneurs and investors with valuable insight into how businesses scale, how public markets function, and how wealth is created through strategic access to capital. Ultimately, companies that succeed in public markets are often those capable of balancing ambition with discipline, growth with governance, and storytelling with operational execution. Capital alone does not guarantee success. What matters most is how effectively companies deploy that capital to create sustainable long-term value for customers, employees, shareholders, and the broader market itself.

The Investors Who Almost Walked Away

Jordan Vale adjusted his tie nervously as the elevator climbed toward the sixty-second floor of the Manhattan office tower. Outside the glass walls, New York stretched endlessly beneath the gray winter sky. Financial institutions, hedge funds, private equity firms, and investment banks filled the city below—each controlling billions of dollars capable of transforming companies overnight.

Today, Jordan needed those billions.

His company, LuminaGrid Systems, had developed advanced smart-grid software designed to optimize energy distribution across national power infrastructures. The technology used artificial intelligence to predict electricity demand, reduce waste, and stabilize renewable energy integration into aging utility systems.

The business had enormous potential.

But potential alone did not pay for expansion.

Three months earlier, LuminaGrid agreed to merge with Apex Horizon Acquisition Corp., a SPAC led by former infrastructure investor Daniel Roth. The transaction valued the company at nearly $5 billion and promised access to hundreds of millions in capital.

At least that was the original plan.

Then market conditions deteriorated.

Interest rates began rising sharply. Investors grew increasingly skeptical of SPAC transactions. Several high-profile companies missed projections, triggering widespread panic throughout the sector.

Now redemption fears threatened the merger itself.

Without additional institutional support, the transaction might collapse entirely.

Jordan entered the conference room where representatives from several major investment firms waited around a massive marble table.

These investors controlled the PIPE financing round that would determine whether LuminaGrid survived.

Daniel Roth leaned toward Jordan quietly before the meeting began. “They’re nervous,” he whispered.

Jordan already knew.

The previous week, two institutional investors withdrew completely after reviewing updated market conditions. Financial media outlets increasingly criticized speculative growth valuations. Public enthusiasm surrounding SPACs was disappearing rapidly.

One investor opened the meeting bluntly.

“Why should we trust your projections when most SPAC companies are collapsing?”

Jordan paused before answering carefully.

“Because our revenue already exists.”

He projected utility contract data across the large presentation screens.

Unlike many speculative technology startups, LuminaGrid already operated commercial systems across multiple regional energy networks. The company generated recurring enterprise revenue and possessed long-term infrastructure contracts.

Still, skepticism remained. Another investor flipped through financial reports.

"Your expansion assumptions are extremely aggressive."

"They're based on actual utility demand trends," Jordan replied calmly.

"But your profitability timeline depends on rapid adoption."

Jordan nodded.

"Yes."

The room fell silent.

Jordan realized something important in that moment: these investors no longer cared about futuristic narratives alone.

They wanted operational certainty.

For the next four hours, the meeting became an intense examination of every aspect of the business. Investors questioned customer retention rates, infrastructure costs, regulatory exposure, cybersecurity risks, hiring plans, and international expansion assumptions.

By the end of the session, Jordan felt emotionally exhausted.

As investors slowly exited the room, one older portfolio manager remained seated quietly.

“My fund survived the dot-com crash,” the man said calmly.

Jordan listened carefully.

“Back then, investors funded almost anything involving the internet,” the manager continued. “Most companies failed.”

Jordan nodded silently.

“But the companies that survived built real infrastructure. They solved real problems.”

The investor closed the financial report slowly.

“That’s what I’m trying to figure out about your company.”

Two weeks later, market conditions worsened further.

SPAC stocks collapsed across the market after several disappointing earnings reports triggered panic selling. Retail investors exited speculative growth positions aggressively. Financial commentators predicted the end of the SPAC era entirely.

Inside LuminaGrid headquarters, employees watched the market chaos anxiously.

"What happens if the PIPE falls apart?" one executive asked during an emergency board meeting.

Jordan stared at updated financing models projected across the conference room screen. "If the institutional funding disappears, the merger likely fails."

The room fell silent.

Years of work suddenly depended on whether investors still believed in the company's future.

Late one evening, Jordan sat alone inside his office reviewing utility infrastructure reports. Outside the building, San Francisco glowed beneath heavy rain clouds.

His phone buzzed.

It was Daniel Roth.

"They want revised terms," Daniel said immediately.

Jordan closed his eyes.

"How bad?"

"Lower valuation. Additional investor protections. More warrants."

Jordan leaned back silently.

Accepting the terms would create major dilution for existing shareholders.

Rejecting them could destroy the deal completely.

For several minutes neither man spoke.

Finally, Jordan asked quietly, "Do you think they still believe in the business?"

Daniel paused.

"I think they're afraid of the market."

That statement changed Jordan's perspective entirely.

The next morning, Jordan gathered the executive team.

"We stop selling hype," he said firmly.

The room looked confused.

"We focus only on operational reality from this point forward."

Over the following days, management revised projections conservatively, reduced speculative growth assumptions, and emphasized existing commercial performance instead of futuristic narratives.

The investor response shifted noticeably.

Confidence slowly improved.

Institutional investors who previously worried about unrealistic expectations began viewing LuminaGrid as a more disciplined infrastructure technology company rather than another speculative SPAC-era growth story.

One week before the merger vote, the PIPE financing round officially closed successfully.

LuminaGrid secured nearly $450 million in institutional capital commitments.

The merger proceeded.

When LuminaGrid began trading publicly, the stock initially performed modestly rather than explosively. Unlike many speculative SPAC deals that surged wildly on excitement, investors treated the company cautiously.

Jordan preferred it that way.

Over the next several years, LuminaGrid expanded steadily across global energy markets. Utility modernization accelerated worldwide as governments invested heavily in renewable infrastructure and grid optimization systems.

Revenue grew consistently.

Profitability improved gradually.

Institutional ownership increased steadily as long-term investors recognized the company's operational strength.

Five years later, LuminaGrid had become one of the largest smart-grid technology providers globally.

During an energy conference in London, a young founder approached Jordan after his presentation.

"How did you convince institutional investors to support your deal during the SPAC crash?" the founder asked.

Jordan smiled thoughtfully.

"We stopped trying to impress them."

The founder looked confused.

"What do you mean?"

Jordan glanced across the crowded conference hall before answering.

"Investors eventually stop paying for excitement alone. They start paying for reality."

Chapter 8

Regulation, Governance, and the Responsibilities of Public Companies

Becoming a publicly traded company is often viewed as one of the greatest achievements in business. Public market access can create liquidity, visibility, institutional credibility, expansion capital, and enormous wealth creation opportunities for founders, employees, and investors. However, many entrepreneurs initially focus so heavily on the excitement of going public that they underestimate the responsibilities and regulatory obligations that accompany life as a public company. The transition from private ownership to public accountability fundamentally changes how a company operates, communicates, manages risk, and interacts with investors.

Public companies do not simply answer to founders or private investors. Once publicly traded, companies become accountable to regulators, institutional investors, retail shareholders, analysts, exchanges, auditors, attorneys, employees, and the broader financial markets. Transparency, governance, compliance, and financial discipline become essential requirements rather than optional business considerations. Understanding these responsibilities is critically important for any founder, executive, or investor involved in alternative public offerings such as SPACs, direct listings, reverse mergers, or traditional IPOs.

One of the primary reasons financial regulations exist is to protect investors and maintain confidence in public markets. Public markets function effectively only when investors believe companies are providing reasonably accurate financial information and operating within established legal standards. Without trust and transparency, capital markets become unstable and investor participation declines.

Throughout financial history, periods of excessive speculation, fraud, accounting manipulation, or weak governance have often triggered regulatory reforms designed to strengthen market integrity. Major corporate scandals involving misleading financial statements, insider trading, conflicts of interest, or deceptive disclosures have repeatedly demonstrated the importance of oversight within public markets.

When a company becomes public, one of its most important responsibilities involves financial reporting. Public companies must provide regular disclosures regarding revenue, expenses, profits, risks, executive compensation, debt obligations, operational performance, and material business developments. In the United States, companies typically file quarterly reports, annual reports, and other required disclosures with the Securities and Exchange Commission.

These filings allow investors to evaluate company performance and make informed investment decisions. Financial transparency therefore becomes one of the foundational principles of public markets. Investors must have access to consistent and reasonably reliable information in order to assess valuation, risk, and future potential effectively.

Preparing these reports requires substantial organizational infrastructure. Public companies often maintain teams of accountants, attorneys, compliance specialists, investor relations professionals, and auditors responsible for ensuring accurate reporting and regulatory compliance. Many private companies underestimate how demanding these requirements become after entering the public markets.

Audits also play a critical role in maintaining investor confidence. Independent accounting firms review financial statements to ensure they conform to accepted accounting standards and accurately reflect the company's financial condition. While audits cannot eliminate all risks or guarantee future performance, they provide an additional layer of oversight intended to reduce fraud and improve transparency.

Governance structures become increasingly important once companies become public. Corporate governance refers to the systems, policies, leadership structures, and oversight mechanisms used to manage and supervise companies responsibly. Strong governance helps protect shareholder interests, improve accountability, and reduce conflicts of interest within management teams.

Public companies typically establish boards of directors responsible for overseeing executive leadership and protecting shareholder interests. These boards often include independent directors with expertise in finance, law, operations, industry strategy, or governance. Independent oversight helps ensure that executives do not operate entirely without accountability or external review.

Board governance becomes especially important during periods of rapid growth, financial stress, or market volatility. Strong boards can provide strategic guidance, operational oversight, and risk management support while helping companies navigate difficult decisions. Weak governance, however, can contribute to poor decision-making, excessive risk-taking, or operational instability.

The rise of SPACs highlighted the importance of governance standards dramatically. During the SPAC boom, some companies entered public markets quickly without fully developing the internal controls, governance systems, or reporting infrastructure typically associated with mature public companies. As market conditions weakened, operational weaknesses and governance problems became more visible.

Several SPAC-era companies faced criticism regarding overly optimistic projections, insufficient disclosure practices, accounting irregularities, or conflicts of interest involving sponsors and executives. These controversies increased regulatory scrutiny and reinforced the importance of transparency and disciplined governance within alternative public offerings.

Conflicts of interest represent another major governance concern. In financial markets, incentives often shape behavior powerfully. Executives may seek compensation tied to stock performance. Sponsors may benefit financially from completing transactions even if long-term outcomes remain uncertain. Investors may pursue short-term gains that conflict with long-term company stability. Effective governance systems attempt to balance these competing incentives responsibly.

Executive compensation also becomes a highly visible issue once companies become public. Public shareholders often evaluate how executives are paid and whether compensation structures align with long-term shareholder interests. Excessive compensation, poorly designed incentive structures, or controversial insider transactions can damage investor confidence significantly.

Insider trading regulations further illustrate the importance of fairness within public markets. Executives, employees, and insiders often possess material non-public information regarding company performance, acquisitions, earnings results, or strategic developments. Trading securities based on confidential information before public disclosure undermines market fairness and investor trust. Regulatory systems therefore impose strict rules regarding insider trading activities and disclosure obligations.

Investor relations become another essential responsibility of public companies. Once publicly traded, companies must communicate regularly with investors, analysts, media outlets, and shareholders. Quarterly earnings calls, investor presentations, annual meetings, press releases, and strategic updates all influence market perception and investor confidence.

Strong communication requires balancing optimism with realism. Companies must explain growth opportunities and strategic vision while also disclosing risks and operational challenges transparently. Overpromising may temporarily support stock prices, but failure to deliver can severely damage credibility later.

Market expectations create constant pressure for public companies. Investors and analysts often evaluate quarterly revenue growth, earnings performance, profit margins, customer metrics, and operational efficiency closely. Companies missing expectations may experience immediate stock price declines even if long-term business fundamentals remain strong.

This short-term pressure can create tension between quarterly market performance and long-term strategic decision-making. Some executives become overly focused on short-term earnings management at the expense of innovation, research, employee development, or long-term infrastructure investment. Successful public companies must balance immediate shareholder expectations with sustainable strategic growth.

Another major responsibility of public companies involves risk disclosure. Public businesses must inform investors about material risks affecting operations, finances, competition, regulation, cybersecurity, supply chains, litigation exposure, economic conditions, and market volatility. Investors cannot evaluate opportunities properly without understanding associated risks. Cybersecurity has become particularly important in modern markets. As businesses increasingly rely on digital infrastructure, cloud systems, artificial intelligence, and global data networks, cybersecurity threats represent major operational and financial risks. Public companies face growing pressure to protect customer data, maintain operational resilience, and disclose cyber-related risks transparently.

Environmental, social, and governance factors, commonly known as ESG considerations, have also become increasingly influential within public markets. Institutional investors increasingly evaluate how companies address environmental sustainability, labor practices, diversity, ethical governance, and social responsibility. Companies ignoring these issues may face reputational damage, investor pressure, or reduced institutional support.

At the same time, critics argue that excessive regulation can create substantial burdens for smaller or emerging public companies. Compliance costs, legal risks, reporting obligations, and governance requirements can consume enormous amounts of time and resources. Some entrepreneurs believe public market regulations discourage innovation or create incentives for companies to remain private longer.

This debate reflects a broader tension within capitalism itself: balancing investor protection with entrepreneurial flexibility. Financial markets require enough regulation to maintain trust and transparency, but excessive complexity may reduce efficiency and innovation. Regulators continually attempt to balance these competing priorities as markets evolve.

Alternative public offerings intensified these discussions because they challenged traditional assumptions regarding how companies enter public markets. SPACs, direct listings, and reverse mergers accelerated access to public investors but also raised concerns regarding whether some companies were becoming public before developing sufficient operational maturity or governance infrastructure.

As a result, regulatory agencies implemented additional scrutiny regarding SPAC accounting standards, disclosure practices, financial projections, and sponsor compensation structures. These changes reflected broader efforts to improve transparency and investor protection within evolving capital market environments.

Public companies must also manage reputational risk carefully. In the digital age, information spreads globally within seconds. Social media, financial news platforms, online communities, and digital investors amplify both positive and negative narratives rapidly. Executive behavior, public statements, operational setbacks, legal disputes, or governance controversies can trigger immediate market reactions. Leadership integrity therefore becomes critically important. Public market investors evaluate not only financial performance but also management credibility, communication quality, strategic consistency, and ethical behavior. Trust remains one of the most valuable assets within capital markets.

For founders transitioning from private to public leadership, these responsibilities often require significant personal adjustment. Private startups frequently operate with flexibility, informality, and rapid decision-making processes. Public companies require greater structure, documentation, accountability, and procedural discipline.

Some founders thrive within public markets by building strong executive teams, governance systems, and operational infrastructure. Others struggle with the constant scrutiny, investor pressure, regulatory obligations, and loss of privacy associated with public leadership roles.

Ultimately, successful public companies understand that governance and compliance are not merely regulatory obligations—they are strategic advantages. Strong governance builds investor confidence, improves operational stability, reduces legal risk, and supports long-term value creation. Transparent companies capable of maintaining trust during difficult periods often outperform those relying primarily on short-term hype or aggressive narratives.

The future of public market regulation will likely continue evolving alongside technological innovation, artificial intelligence, decentralized finance systems, blockchain infrastructure, and global digital investing platforms. Regulators will continue adapting oversight mechanisms to address new risks, financial structures, and market behaviors.

However, regardless of how markets evolve technologically, the core principles underlying successful public companies will likely remain consistent: transparency, accountability, integrity, disciplined execution, and responsible leadership.

Public markets create extraordinary opportunities for wealth creation and business expansion, but they also require companies to operate within systems designed to protect investors and maintain market confidence. Founders and investors who understand these responsibilities will be better positioned to navigate public markets intelligently and build sustainable long-term enterprises capable of surviving beyond temporary market cycles or speculative enthusiasm.

The Price of Transparency

Evelyn Carter sat quietly at the head of the boardroom table while attorneys, auditors, and executives argued around her. Financial reports covered every screen in the room. Outside the windows, Boston glowed beneath a cold December snowfall, but inside the headquarters of Synexis Biotech, the atmosphere felt suffocating.

Three years earlier, Evelyn's company became one of the most celebrated healthcare SPAC mergers in the country.

Now regulators were investigating them.

When Synexis first entered public markets, everything moved quickly.

The company developed advanced gene-editing therapies designed to treat rare neurological diseases. Early clinical trials generated promising results, and investors became obsessed with the company's long-term potential.

A healthcare-focused SPAC called Horizon Life Sciences Acquisition Corp. approached Synexis with a merger proposal valuing the company at over $7 billion.

At the time, the valuation felt like a miracle.

Synexis still operated with limited commercial revenue. Drug development remained expensive and uncertain. Regulatory approvals could take years.

But investors loved the story.

Gene-editing technology represented one of the hottest sectors in the market. Analysts described Synexis as a revolutionary company capable of transforming modern medicine.

After the merger closed, the stock surged dramatically.

Financial media outlets celebrated Evelyn as a visionary scientist-turned-CEO. Magazine covers described her as "The Future of Biotechnology." Institutional investors aggressively accumulated shares.

For a while, everything seemed perfect.

Then reality arrived.

Clinical trials experienced delays. Research costs increased sharply. Regulatory questions emerged regarding long-term treatment safety. Revenue timelines shifted further into the future.

Public market pressure intensified almost immediately.

Analysts demanded constant updates regarding trial progress. Investors expected aggressive timelines and breakthrough announcements. Financial media scrutinized every company statement carefully.

Inside Synexis, operational stress grew rapidly. “We need more optimistic guidance,” one board member insisted during an executive meeting.

“Our data isn’t strong enough yet,” Evelyn replied firmly.

“But the market expects progress.”

Evelyn understood the pressure.

The stock price had become central to everything. Employee morale depended on it. Institutional investors monitored it constantly. Future fundraising capability depended on maintaining market confidence.

Gradually, internal communication became more aggressive.

Executives debated whether certain clinical developments should be described more positively during investor presentations. Public relations teams crafted increasingly optimistic language regarding future milestones.

Evelyn felt increasingly uncomfortable.

One evening, the company's general counsel entered her office carrying a folder filled with regulatory correspondence.

"The SEC is asking questions about our investor disclosures," he said carefully.

Evelyn stared at him silently.

"What kind of questions?"

"They believe some of our forward projections may have lacked sufficient risk disclosure."

The room became painfully quiet.

Over the following months, regulators expanded their investigation. Auditors reviewed financial reporting processes extensively. Attorneys analyzed public statements, investor presentations, and internal communications.

Financial media quickly learned about the investigation.

Headlines exploded across the market.

"Former SPAC Biotech Company Under Federal Review."

"Questions Emerge About Synexis Projections."

The stock collapsed.

Investors panicked. Analysts downgraded the company aggressively. Online traders mocked the entire SPAC healthcare sector once again.

Inside headquarters, employees looked terrified.

Many joined Synexis believing they were helping revolutionize medicine while building long-term financial security through stock ownership. Now their options were collapsing in value as uncertainty consumed the company.

During one brutal board meeting, tensions exploded openly.

"We should have never gone public this early," one director argued.

"We needed the capital," another replied.

"But we weren't operationally ready."

Evelyn remained silent while the arguments continued around her.

Deep down, she knew both sides were correct.

The company genuinely needed public capital to continue research and development.

But the pressures of public markets had gradually distorted decision-making throughout the organization.

Instead of focusing entirely on scientific execution, management became increasingly focused on investor perception.

The investigation lasted nearly a year. Ultimately, regulators did not accuse Synexis of fraud, but they criticized the company's disclosure practices and required substantial governance reforms, expanded risk disclosures, and enhanced compliance procedures.

The financial damage, however, had already occurred.

Institutional confidence weakened significantly. The stock remained far below its peak valuation. Several executives resigned. Recruiting top talent became more difficult.

For a period, Evelyn considered resigning herself.

Then one afternoon, she walked quietly through the company's research laboratory and stopped beside a young scientist working late alone.

The researcher looked up nervously.

"Sorry, I didn't realize anyone else was still here."

Evelyn smiled faintly.

"What are you working on?"

The scientist explained the latest trial results carefully.

As Evelyn listened, she realized something important.

Despite all the financial chaos, the science itself still mattered. The mission remained real.

That realization changed her leadership approach completely.

Over the next several years, Synexis transformed internally. Governance systems strengthened dramatically. Compliance infrastructure expanded. Investor communication became more disciplined and transparent. Management stopped emphasizing aggressive timelines and focused instead on operational reality.

The process was painful and slow.

But gradually, investor trust began returning.

Clinical progress continued steadily. Research quality improved. Regulatory relationships stabilized. Institutional investors once again viewed Synexis as a serious biotechnology company rather than simply another speculative SPAC-era growth story.

Years later, during a healthcare innovation conference, a young biotech founder approached Evelyn after her keynote speech.

"What's the biggest lesson you learned from becoming public?" the founder asked.

Evelyn thought quietly before answering.

"Public markets don't just measure performance," she said. "They measure trust."

The founder nodded carefully.

"And once trust breaks?"

Evelyn looked toward the crowded conference hall.

"You spend years earning it back."

Chapter 9

Building Long-Term Wealth Through Public Companies and Equity Ownership

One of the most powerful wealth creation mechanisms in modern history has been equity ownership. While salaries, commissions, and short-term business income can create financial stability, long-term wealth has often been built through ownership of appreciating assets. Public companies, in particular, have generated extraordinary fortunes for founders, employees, investors, and institutions because equity ownership allows individuals to participate directly in business growth, market expansion, innovation, and increasing valuations over time.

Understanding how equity ownership creates wealth is essential for entrepreneurs, investors, executives, and employees navigating public markets and alternative public offerings. Whether through traditional IPOs, SPAC mergers, direct listings, or reverse mergers, becoming publicly traded creates opportunities for liquidity, valuation growth, capital appreciation, and generational wealth creation that private ownership alone may not always provide. Many people mistakenly believe that wealthy founders become rich primarily because they receive large salaries after taking companies public. In reality, salaries often represent only a small portion of long-term founder wealth. The majority of substantial wealth creation usually comes from ownership stakes in businesses whose valuations increase dramatically over time.

When a founder owns a meaningful percentage of a company valued at millions or billions of dollars, the underlying equity itself becomes the primary source of wealth. If a company's valuation grows from ten million dollars to one billion dollars, even a modest ownership percentage can create life-changing financial outcomes. This principle applies not only to founders but also to early employees, investors, executives, and shareholders who participate in the company's growth journey.

Public markets amplify this wealth creation process because they provide liquidity and continuous valuation mechanisms. Private companies may possess significant theoretical value, but converting that value into accessible financial wealth often requires a liquidity event such as an IPO, acquisition, SPAC merger, or public listing. Once shares become publicly tradable, shareholders gain the ability to buy, sell, borrow against, or diversify their equity positions more efficiently.

One reason equity ownership is so powerful is because it allows wealth to scale nonlinearly. Traditional employment income is usually tied directly to time and labor. Equity ownership, however, can appreciate exponentially if a business grows successfully. This creates leverage through ownership rather than through hourly productivity alone.

Technology entrepreneurs provide some of the clearest examples of this phenomenon. Many founders initially earned modest salaries while building companies privately. Their wealth expanded dramatically only after their businesses achieved scale and public market valuations increased substantially. Early employees holding stock options often experienced similar outcomes as their ownership stakes appreciated alongside company growth.

Public companies also create opportunities for ordinary investors to participate in long-term wealth creation. Through stock ownership, retail investors gain exposure to industries, technologies, and businesses capable of expanding globally over time. Investors who identify strong companies early and maintain disciplined long-term positions may benefit from compounding growth over decades.

Compounding represents one of the most important concepts in long-term investing. When companies grow earnings, revenues, cash flow, and market share consistently over time, shareholder value may increase exponentially through reinvestment and appreciation. Small ownership stakes in exceptional businesses can become extremely valuable over long periods if growth continues steadily.

However, building wealth through public markets requires patience, discipline, emotional control, and strategic thinking. Financial markets fluctuate constantly due to economic cycles, investor psychology, interest rates, geopolitical events, technological disruption, and competitive pressures. Short-term volatility can create fear and emotional decision-making that undermines long-term wealth accumulation.

Many investors lose money not because they selected poor companies initially, but because they reacted emotionally during market downturns. Fear often causes investors to sell strong businesses during temporary declines, while greed may encourage excessive speculation during euphoric market periods. Successful long-term investors typically develop the ability to remain disciplined despite market volatility.

Alternative public offerings such as SPACs highlighted both the opportunities and dangers associated with equity-based wealth creation. During the SPAC boom, many founders, early investors, and retail traders experienced dramatic increases in paper wealth as valuations surged rapidly. However, when market conditions changed, many speculative valuations collapsed equally quickly.

This cycle reinforced an important distinction between paper wealth and realized wealth. Public market valuations fluctuate continuously. A founder may appear extremely wealthy based on market capitalization, but that wealth remains partially theoretical until shares are sold, diversified, or converted into other assets. Sharp market declines can reduce paper wealth dramatically even when businesses continue operating successfully.

Liquidity management therefore becomes critically important after companies become public. Founders, executives, and early investors must decide when to hold shares, when to diversify, and how to balance long-term confidence with risk management. Concentrated ownership positions may create enormous upside potential, but they also expose individuals to significant volatility if company valuations decline.

Many successful founders eventually diversify portions of their wealth into other assets such as real estate, private businesses, index funds, bonds, venture investments, infrastructure, or cash reserves. Diversification helps reduce dependence on the performance of a single company or industry while preserving long-term financial stability. Tax planning also becomes increasingly important as equity wealth grows. Public company stock sales, options exercises, restricted stock units, and liquidity events often create significant tax consequences. Wealthy founders and investors typically work closely with tax professionals, estate planners, attorneys, and financial advisors to structure transactions efficiently and preserve long-term wealth.

Another major advantage of public equity ownership involves access to leverage and financial flexibility. Public shares can often serve as collateral for loans, lines of credit, acquisitions, or additional investments. Wealthy individuals sometimes borrow against appreciated stock positions rather than selling shares immediately, allowing them to maintain ownership while accessing liquidity simultaneously.

This strategy can support entrepreneurship, real estate investing, private equity participation, or lifestyle flexibility without triggering immediate taxable events. However, leverage also introduces risk because declining share prices may create margin pressure or forced asset sales during volatile market conditions.

Employee equity compensation represents another important wealth creation mechanism within public companies. Stock options, restricted stock units, performance shares, and employee stock purchase plans allow workers to participate directly in company growth. In many successful technology companies, employees accumulated substantial wealth through equity participation despite relatively modest initial salaries.

Equity compensation also aligns incentives between employees and shareholders. Workers who benefit from increasing company value may become more motivated to support long-term business success. However, employees must understand the risks associated with concentrated stock ownership and speculative valuations.

The psychology of wealth creation through public markets is also important. Rapid financial success can create emotional challenges, overconfidence, lifestyle inflation, and distorted decision-making. Many individuals who suddenly become wealthy through public offerings struggle with maintaining discipline, managing risk, and preserving wealth long term.

History contains countless examples of founders and investors who accumulated enormous paper fortunes during speculative booms only to lose substantial wealth later through excessive leverage, poor diversification, overconfidence, or market collapses. Sustainable wealth management requires balancing ambition with discipline and risk awareness.

At the same time, long-term equity ownership remains one of the most effective methods for building generational wealth. Public markets allow ownership participation in businesses capable of global scale and long-term growth. Companies that successfully adapt to changing industries, innovate consistently, and maintain competitive advantages may create extraordinary shareholder value over decades.

Many of the world's wealthiest individuals accumulated fortunes through long-term ownership rather than short-term trading. They benefited from compounding business growth, reinvestment, operational scalability, and expanding market valuations over extended periods. Patience often proved more valuable than constant speculation.

Understanding market cycles is essential within this process. Bull markets may create rapid appreciation and widespread optimism, while bear markets often produce fear and sharp declines. Long-term wealth builders typically recognize that volatility is natural within financial systems. Rather than reacting emotionally to short-term fluctuations, they focus on underlying business fundamentals and long-term positioning.

Public company founders face additional complexities because their personal wealth often remains closely tied to company performance. Balancing leadership responsibilities with personal financial planning can become difficult, particularly during volatile periods. Founders may feel pressure to maintain confidence publicly even while managing personal financial uncertainty privately.

Another important aspect of long-term wealth creation involves legacy. Public companies capable of sustained growth may create opportunities not only for founders but also for employees, communities, pension funds, retirement accounts, and future generations of investors. Equity ownership therefore influences broader economic systems beyond individual financial outcomes alone.

Public markets also democratize wealth creation opportunities to some extent. Ordinary investors can purchase shares in companies shaping global industries and technological innovation. While risks remain significant, public ownership structures allow broader participation in economic growth compared to purely private financial systems.

The future of equity ownership may evolve significantly as financial technology advances. Blockchain systems, tokenized securities, decentralized finance platforms, artificial intelligence-driven investing tools, and global digital asset markets may transform how ownership is distributed and traded. Fractional ownership structures may increase accessibility further. Nevertheless, the core principle underlying long-term wealth creation will likely remain consistent: ownership of productive assets capable of generating sustainable value over time. Public markets simply provide one of the most scalable systems for facilitating that ownership globally.

For entrepreneurs, understanding equity ownership can reshape how businesses are structured from the earliest stages. Ownership percentages, dilution management, capital raising strategy, employee compensation, and governance decisions all influence long-term wealth outcomes substantially. Small ownership differences early in a company's lifecycle can translate into enormous financial differences later.

For investors, understanding equity-based wealth creation encourages patience, discipline, and long-term thinking. Chasing short-term hype often produces inconsistent results, while identifying sustainable businesses with strong leadership and scalable economics may generate compounding returns over decades.

Ultimately, building long-term wealth through public companies requires more than simply becoming public. It requires creating businesses capable of delivering sustainable value through changing economic conditions, competitive environments, technological shifts, and market cycles. Public offerings create opportunity, but operational execution determines whether that opportunity evolves into lasting wealth.

The individuals who succeed most consistently within public markets often understand that wealth creation is not merely about stock prices. It is about ownership, discipline, strategic positioning, risk management, adaptability, and long-term value creation. Those principles remain central regardless of how financial markets evolve in the future.

The Shares He Never Sold

Nathan Cole sat quietly on the balcony of his Miami beachfront condominium watching the sunrise spread across the Atlantic Ocean. Waves rolled steadily against the shore while financial news played softly from the television inside the living room.

Another market rally was pushing technology stocks to record highs.

His phone buzzed repeatedly with notifications from financial advisors, journalists, and investors requesting interviews.

But Nathan ignored them all.

At fifty-eight years old, he no longer cared much about headlines.

What fascinated him now was how impossible his life once seemed.

Thirty years earlier, Nathan worked as a software engineer living in a tiny apartment outside Austin, Texas. He spent nights writing code for a small startup called HorizonLink Networks while struggling to pay monthly rent.

Back then, the company had only twelve employees and almost no outside funding.

Most people believed the internet itself was little more than a passing trend.

Nathan remembered one particular night clearly.

The founder, Eric Dawson, gathered the small team inside a cramped conference room with stained carpets and broken chairs.

"We can't afford large salaries," Eric admitted nervously. "But I can offer stock options."

Most employees barely understood what stock options even meant.

Several workers left the company within months seeking higher-paying jobs elsewhere.

Nathan stayed. Not because he believed he would become wealthy.

He simply believed in the product they were building.

Years passed slowly.

The company struggled constantly. Investors rejected them repeatedly. Competitors with larger funding rounds entered the market aggressively. Several times HorizonLink nearly collapsed financially.

Nathan often questioned whether staying had been a mistake.

Then everything changed.

The internet exploded globally.

Demand for HorizonLink's infrastructure software accelerated beyond anything management expected. Venture capital poured into technology markets. Revenues surged rapidly.

Suddenly, the same investors who once ignored the company desperately wanted ownership.

Eventually, HorizonLink went public through a traditional IPO during the late stages of the technology boom.

On listing day, Nathan watched the stock price rise so rapidly that employees inside headquarters began cheering wildly.

Financial news anchors described HorizonLink as one of the most promising internet infrastructure companies in the world.

Overnight, Nathan became worth millions on paper.

Friends who previously questioned his career choices suddenly treated him differently. Banks offered private wealth management services. Luxury real estate agents began contacting him constantly.

But Nathan made one unusual decision.

He refused to sell most of his shares.

Financial advisors warned him repeatedly about concentration risk.

"You need diversification," one advisor insisted.

Nathan understood the logic.

But he also understood the company itself better than almost anyone.

While many early employees sold aggressively during the initial excitement, Nathan quietly continued holding the majority of his position.

Then came the dot-com crash.

Technology stocks collapsed across global markets.

Companies that once traded at absurd valuations disappeared entirely within months. Investors panicked. Financial media declared the internet boom dead.

HorizonLink's stock fell nearly eighty percent.

Nathan watched millions of dollars vanish from his account statements.

Friends told him he was crazy for not selling earlier.

"You should have cashed out," people repeated constantly.

But Nathan still refused to panic.

Unlike many speculative technology companies, HorizonLink possessed real infrastructure, recurring enterprise customers, and growing long-term demand.

The business itself remained strong despite market fear.

Over the next decade, the internet transformed global commerce exactly as HorizonLink originally predicted. Data infrastructure demand exploded worldwide. Cloud computing expanded rapidly. Enterprise software became essential across every major industry. Slowly, HorizonLink recovered. Then it expanded.

Then it dominated globally.

By the time Nathan reached his fifties, his remaining ownership stake had grown into a fortune far larger than anything he imagined during the IPO years earlier.

But the most important lesson was not the money itself.

It was understanding how wealth actually grows.

Nathan realized most people focus too heavily on short-term price movements instead of long-term ownership.

During market crashes, fear convinces investors that temporary declines represent permanent destruction. During bull markets, greed convinces people that prices can only continue rising forever.

Both emotions distort judgment.

One afternoon, Nathan visited HorizonLink headquarters for the company's thirtieth anniversary celebration. Thousands of employees filled the campus auditorium while executives discussed the company's global expansion.

After the event, a young software engineer approached him nervously.

"Is it true you still own most of your original shares?" the employee asked.

Nathan smiled slightly.

"Most of them."

The engineer looked stunned.

"How did you hold through all the crashes?"

Nathan thought quietly before answering.

"Because I stopped thinking like a trader."

The employee looked confused.

“What do you mean?”

Nathan pointed toward the giant HorizonLink logo displayed across the auditorium stage.

“I wasn’t holding a stock symbol,” he explained. “I was holding ownership in a business I believed would matter for decades.”

The engineer nodded slowly.

Nathan continued.

“Markets move emotionally every day. But long-term wealth usually belongs to the people who stay focused on the business itself while everyone else gets distracted by fear and excitement.”

Chapter 10

The Future of Public Markets, Innovation, and Global Wealth Creation

The world of finance is entering one of the most transformative periods in modern history. Technology, globalization, artificial intelligence, decentralized systems, digital assets, and evolving investor behavior are reshaping how companies raise capital, how ownership is distributed, and how wealth is created worldwide. Public markets, once dominated primarily by traditional stock exchanges, institutional gatekeepers, and legacy financial systems, are evolving into faster, more interconnected, more technology-driven ecosystems capable of reaching billions of participants globally.

The rise of SPACs, direct listings, reverse mergers, and alternative public offerings represented only the beginning of this transformation. These structures challenged long-standing assumptions about how businesses should access capital and public investors. They demonstrated that entrepreneurs and financial markets are willing to innovate aggressively when traditional systems become inefficient, restrictive, or misaligned with modern economic realities. As technology continues advancing, the future of public markets may look dramatically different from the systems investors recognize today. Yet despite these changes, the underlying drivers of wealth creation—ownership, innovation, scalability, capital access, and human ambition—will likely remain central to the global economy for decades to come.

One of the most important forces shaping the future of public markets is technological acceleration. Throughout history, major technological shifts have repeatedly created new industries, new forms of capital formation, and new opportunities for wealth creation. Railroads, industrial manufacturing, telecommunications, automobiles, computing, the internet, mobile technology, and cloud infrastructure all transformed financial systems alongside broader economic activity.

Artificial intelligence may become the next major technological revolution capable of reshaping capital markets fundamentally. AI systems are already influencing trading algorithms, investment analysis, fraud detection, risk management, financial forecasting, regulatory compliance, customer service, and operational automation across the financial sector. As AI capabilities continue advancing, public companies may operate more efficiently while investors gain access to increasingly sophisticated analytical tools. AI-driven financial systems may eventually reduce information asymmetry within markets by allowing broader access to advanced research and predictive modeling previously available primarily to large institutions. Retail investors could gain tools capable of analyzing earnings reports, industry trends, market sentiment, and valuation models in real time using artificial intelligence platforms.

At the same time, AI may increase market complexity and volatility. Algorithmic trading systems already execute enormous volumes of transactions automatically across global exchanges. As automation becomes more advanced, market reactions may occur faster and with greater intensity than ever before. Investors and regulators alike will need to adapt to increasingly machine-driven financial environments.

Blockchain technology and decentralized finance systems also represent major forces shaping the future of public markets. Blockchain infrastructure enables digital ownership verification, decentralized transaction processing, and tokenized asset systems capable of operating globally without relying entirely on traditional intermediaries.

Tokenization refers to the process of converting ownership rights in assets into digital tokens tradable on blockchain networks. In the future, stocks, real estate, private equity interests, intellectual property rights, infrastructure assets, commodities, and even revenue streams may become tokenized and traded more efficiently across decentralized marketplaces.

This transformation could significantly increase market accessibility and liquidity. Investors worldwide may eventually purchase fractional ownership stakes in companies or assets instantly through digital platforms operating continuously across global markets. Barriers separating private and public markets could diminish as ownership systems become more flexible and technologically integrated.

Traditional IPOs themselves may evolve substantially. Instead of relying heavily on centralized investment banks and exchange systems, future companies may conduct hybrid digital offerings where institutional and retail investors participate simultaneously through decentralized platforms. Smart contracts may automate portions of regulatory compliance, ownership transfer, dividend distribution, and governance voting processes.

Decentralized finance, commonly called DeFi, may also influence how businesses raise capital. DeFi systems allow financial transactions such as lending, borrowing, staking, trading, and liquidity provision to occur directly through blockchain protocols rather than traditional banking institutions. While still evolving, these systems represent early attempts to create alternative global financial infrastructure. Some entrepreneurs believe future companies may raise growth capital through tokenized ownership structures without relying entirely on traditional exchanges or underwriting systems. Investors worldwide could potentially fund businesses directly through digital capital formation platforms operating continuously across borders.

However, these innovations also introduce significant risks and challenges. Regulation, cybersecurity, fraud prevention, investor protection, identity verification, market manipulation, and legal enforceability remain major concerns within decentralized financial systems. Just as alternative public offerings required evolving regulatory oversight, future digital capital markets will likely require new governance frameworks balancing innovation with stability and investor protection.

Globalization will continue shaping public markets as well. Companies today operate in increasingly interconnected economic systems where customers, investors, employees, suppliers, and competitors often span multiple countries simultaneously. Public markets increasingly reflect this global integration.

Emerging economies are producing rapidly growing

technology companies, financial platforms, manufacturing networks, renewable energy systems, and digital infrastructure businesses capable of competing internationally. As access to capital expands globally, wealth creation opportunities may become more geographically distributed than in previous generations.

At the same time, geopolitical tensions, regulatory fragmentation, trade conflicts, and economic competition between nations may influence future capital flows significantly. Governments increasingly recognize that technology leadership, artificial intelligence capabilities, semiconductor production, cybersecurity infrastructure, and digital financial systems carry strategic importance beyond simple economics.

Public companies operating globally will therefore face increasingly complex environments involving regulatory compliance across multiple jurisdictions, geopolitical risk management, cybersecurity challenges, and international investor relations.

Another major shift involves retail investor participation. Digital brokerages, mobile investing platforms, online financial communities, and social media transformed how ordinary individuals interact with public markets. Millions of retail investors now participate directly in financial markets with unprecedented speed and access to information.

This democratization of investing expanded opportunities but also increased volatility and speculative behavior during certain market periods. Meme stocks, social media-driven trading frenzies, and online investment movements demonstrated how rapidly collective retail sentiment can influence public markets.

Future capital markets will likely continue integrating institutional sophistication with mass retail participation. Investors may gain access to increasingly personalized financial tools, AI-driven portfolio management systems, and decentralized ownership opportunities previously unavailable outside elite financial institutions.

Entrepreneurship itself is evolving alongside these financial changes. Modern startups can scale globally far faster than businesses from previous generations due to cloud computing, digital marketing, artificial intelligence, remote work systems, global payment infrastructure, and software automation. Small teams can now build companies capable of reaching millions of customers worldwide within relatively short periods.

This scalability increases the importance of capital access dramatically. Companies capable of securing financing quickly may achieve winner-take-all advantages in certain industries where network effects, platform dominance, or data accumulation create strong competitive barriers.

Alternative public offerings emerged partly because entrepreneurs sought faster, more flexible methods for accessing growth capital in these accelerated environments. Future financing systems will likely continue evolving to accommodate increasingly rapid business scaling and global competition.

Yet despite all technological and financial innovation, one reality remains consistent: businesses must still create real value.

Public markets may become more decentralized, digital, and automated, but investors will continue evaluating whether companies solve meaningful problems, generate sustainable demand, allocate capital intelligently, and execute strategically over time. Technology may change how ownership is transferred, but it cannot eliminate the importance of operational excellence.

The future will likely produce both extraordinary wealth creation and significant financial volatility. Emerging technologies often generate speculative cycles as investors attempt to predict which innovations will dominate future industries. Some companies will achieve enormous valuations based on transformative breakthroughs. Others will fail despite substantial early enthusiasm.

Understanding this dynamic remains essential for both founders and investors. Technological revolutions create opportunity, but they also produce uncertainty, competition, and rapid change. Long-term success usually belongs not merely to those chasing trends, but to those capable of adapting continuously while maintaining strategic discipline.

The concept of ownership itself may evolve as well. Younger generations increasingly participate in digital economies involving creators, online communities, decentralized organizations, virtual assets, gaming ecosystems, and digital intellectual property. Financial markets may eventually integrate more directly with these emerging economic systems.

Some futurists predict that decentralized autonomous organizations, tokenized communities, AI-managed investment funds, and blockchain-governed enterprises may eventually challenge traditional corporate structures. While many of these ideas remain experimental today, they reflect broader shifts toward increasingly digital and distributed economic participation.

Environmental sustainability will also influence future public markets significantly. Climate change, renewable energy transitions, resource management, and environmental regulation are already reshaping industries globally. Investors increasingly evaluate environmental risks and sustainability strategies when allocating capital. Companies capable of adapting successfully to sustainability-focused economies may attract substantial long-term investment support, while businesses ignoring environmental transitions may face increasing operational and regulatory pressure.

The future of wealth creation may therefore involve combining technological innovation, sustainability, global scalability, financial discipline, and adaptive leadership simultaneously.

For founders, this future presents enormous opportunities alongside substantial responsibilities. Public markets can accelerate business growth and create generational wealth, but they also amplify operational weaknesses, leadership failures, governance problems, and strategic mistakes rapidly.

For investors, future markets may provide broader access to innovation and ownership than any previous era in history. However, abundance of opportunity will also require greater discipline, critical thinking, and long-term strategic judgment. Information overload and speculative hype may become even more intense as digital systems accelerate market communication globally.

One of the most valuable lessons from studying alternative public offerings is understanding that financial systems constantly evolve while human behavior remains surprisingly consistent. Fear, greed, optimism, ambition, speculation, discipline, and innovation continue shaping markets generation after generation.

Technologies may change. Financial structures may evolve. Exchanges may digitize. Ownership systems may decentralize.

But the underlying principles of wealth creation remain remarkably durable.

Ownership matters.

Execution matters.

Adaptability matters.

Trust matters.

Long-term thinking matters.

The future of public markets will likely reward those capable of balancing technological innovation with operational discipline, ambitious vision with realistic execution, and growth opportunities with intelligent risk management.

Ultimately, the future belongs not simply to companies capable of becoming public, but to businesses capable of creating enduring value within rapidly changing global systems. Public offerings, whether through SPACs, direct listings, tokenized assets, or future structures not yet invented, represent tools for accessing capital and opportunity. What determines lasting success is how effectively entrepreneurs, investors, and organizations use those tools to build sustainable enterprises capable of surviving beyond temporary market excitement.

The evolution of capital markets is far from complete. The next generation of entrepreneurs, investors, and innovators may participate in financial systems more interconnected, digital, intelligent, and globally accessible than anything seen before. Those who understand both the opportunities and risks within these transformations may position themselves to help shape the future of global wealth creation itself.

The Company That Went Public Without Wall Street

Lucas Bennett stood inside a dark warehouse in Austin, Texas, staring at the massive holographic display projected across the center of the room. Thousands of glowing data points floated in midair representing investors connected from over ninety countries simultaneously.

In exactly one hour, his company would attempt something no major business had ever accomplished successfully before.

They were going public without Wall Street.

No investment banks.

No traditional stock exchange. No centralized underwriting process.

No institutional gatekeepers controlling allocations.

Everything would happen digitally through a blockchain-based ownership platform accessible globally in real time.

The financial media called it reckless.

Lucas believed it was inevitable.

His company, NexusGrid AI, built decentralized artificial intelligence infrastructure designed to power next-generation financial systems, logistics networks, and autonomous industrial platforms. Over the previous seven years, the business expanded rapidly through private funding and global enterprise partnerships.

By the time NexusGrid prepared for public markets, the company already generated billions in annual revenue.

But Lucas deeply distrusted traditional financial systems.

He spent years studying how IPOs, SPACs, and institutional allocations often concentrated ownership among powerful funds long before ordinary investors gained meaningful access. He believed financial markets remained unnecessarily centralized and inefficient. So NexusGrid built something different.

Using blockchain verification systems, digital ownership tokens, AI-driven compliance automation, and decentralized investor onboarding technology, the company designed a fully global digital public offering system.

Anyone meeting regulatory requirements could participate directly.

Financial regulators initially resisted aggressively.

Major banks criticized the model publicly.

Television analysts warned the system would create chaos, fraud risks, and uncontrollable volatility.

But younger investors worldwide loved the concept.

Millions registered for participation within weeks.

Now, standing inside the warehouse command center, Lucas watched engineers monitor real-time investor verification systems across enormous screens.

His CFO, Maya Chen, approached nervously.

"Regulators approved the final compliance framework," she said.

Lucas nodded slowly.

"And liquidity?"

"Massive."

Outside the building, financial journalists crowded the streets waiting for updates. Social media exploded globally as investors debated whether NexusGrid's offering represented the future of finance or a dangerous experiment.

At exactly 9:00 a.m. Eastern Time, the system activated.

Instantly, ownership orders flooded in globally.

Investors from Singapore, Germany, Brazil, South Korea, Canada, Nigeria, India, and dozens of other countries purchased digital equity tokens directly through the platform. AI systems verified identity, compliance, and transaction settlement automatically in seconds.

No traditional exchange floor existed.

No opening bell rang.

Yet within minutes, billions of dollars in ownership transferred globally.

Financial media reacted with disbelief.

"This may permanently change capital markets," one analyst admitted live on television.

By the end of the first trading day, NexusGrid reached a valuation exceeding $120 billion.

But unlike many speculative public offerings, the company's business itself remained exceptionally strong operationally. AI infrastructure demand accelerated globally while decentralized financial systems expanded rapidly.

Over the next several years, other companies began adopting similar digital public offering structures. Traditional exchanges adapted slowly while regulatory systems evolved to accommodate increasingly decentralized ownership models.

Wall Street itself transformed.

Some legacy institutions resisted.

Others adapted aggressively.

Lucas became one of the most controversial financial figures in the world. Critics accused him of destabilizing traditional finance. Supporters described him as the architect of the next generation of global capital markets.

Yet despite the enormous financial success, Lucas remained focused on one idea above everything else. Access.

He believed ownership opportunities should become globally accessible rather than concentrated among financial elites.

One evening, years later, Lucas stood on a rooftop overlooking Singapore's skyline after speaking at a global finance summit. A young entrepreneur approached him quietly.

"Do you think traditional stock markets will disappear completely?" the founder asked.

Lucas smiled thoughtfully.

"No."

The entrepreneur looked surprised.

"Why not?"

"Because financial systems never disappear all at once," Lucas explained. "They evolve."

The founder nodded slowly.

Lucas looked across the glowing skyline before continuing.

"The future of public markets isn't about destroying ownership systems. It's about expanding access to them."

The young founder stared at the city lights silently. Lucas smiled slightly.

"And that changes everything."

Final IPO Thoughts

The journey through SPACs, reverse mergers, direct listings, institutional financing, market cycles, governance structures, investor psychology, and equity ownership ultimately reveals one important truth: public markets are not simply financial systems. They are engines of transformation capable of changing companies, industries, economies, and individual lives on a massive scale. Alternative public offerings represent far more than technical financial strategies. They symbolize the evolving relationship between entrepreneurship, capital, innovation, and wealth creation in the modern world.

Throughout this book, one consistent theme has appeared repeatedly: going public is not the finish line. It is the beginning of an entirely new phase of responsibility, opportunity, pressure, and strategic decision-making. Many entrepreneurs initially view public market access primarily as a liquidity event or validation milestone. While those elements certainly matter, successful public companies ultimately survive because they continue executing operationally long after the excitement of the public offering fades.

The rise of SPACs and alternative public offerings demonstrated how rapidly financial markets can evolve when investors seek new forms of growth, access, and innovation. For decades, traditional IPOs dominated public market entry almost exclusively. Then new structures emerged that challenged conventional assumptions about how companies should raise capital and achieve liquidity. SPACs accelerated access to public markets. Direct listings reduced reliance on traditional underwriting systems. Reverse mergers provided alternative pathways for smaller or rapidly growing businesses. Each structure reflected changing market conditions and entrepreneurial demands.

Yet despite these innovations, the deeper principles underlying successful companies never truly changed.

Public markets eventually reward businesses capable of delivering real value. Operational discipline, strong leadership, scalable economics, customer demand, financial transparency, governance quality, and strategic adaptability remain the foundations of long-term success regardless of how companies initially become public. Financial engineering alone cannot replace sustainable business execution.

One of the most important lessons from the alternative public offering era is the distinction between excitement and substance. During strong bull markets, investors often become captivated by narratives surrounding disruption, innovation, and future potential. Exciting stories can drive enormous valuations temporarily. Media attention, social momentum, and speculative enthusiasm may accelerate capital flows rapidly into emerging sectors and companies.

However, market psychology eventually shifts.

Public markets are emotional systems influenced by fear, greed, optimism, and uncertainty. Bull markets create confidence and aggressive risk-taking. Bear markets create caution and skepticism. Companies that depend entirely on hype or unrealistic projections often struggle once investor sentiment changes. Businesses grounded in operational strength and long-term strategic execution are more likely to survive volatility and create lasting shareholder value.

This reality explains why some companies emerging from SPACs or alternative public offerings became successful global enterprises while others collapsed after market enthusiasm faded. The structure itself was never the determining factor. What mattered most was the quality of the underlying business, the discipline of leadership, and the company's ability to execute consistently under public market pressure.

Another major lesson involves the extraordinary power of equity ownership. Public markets create one of the most scalable wealth creation systems ever developed because they allow individuals to participate directly in business growth. Founders, employees, investors, and shareholders all gain opportunities to build wealth through ownership rather than solely through labor or salary income.

Equity ownership transforms incentives. It aligns individuals with long-term company performance and creates opportunities for exponential financial growth if businesses succeed. Some of the greatest fortunes in modern history were built not through wages but through ownership stakes in companies that expanded globally over time.

At the same time, equity ownership introduces important responsibilities regarding risk management, diversification, liquidity planning, and emotional discipline. Public market wealth can fluctuate dramatically across economic cycles. Paper fortunes may rise quickly during speculative periods and decline just as rapidly during market corrections. Sustainable long-term wealth requires patience, discipline, and strategic decision-making rather than emotional reactions to short-term volatility.

For founders, the transition from private entrepreneur to public company leader often represents a profound personal transformation. Public markets demand transparency, governance, communication discipline, regulatory compliance, and accountability at levels many private startups never previously experienced. Leadership becomes more visible, more scrutinized, and more consequential once companies become public.

Some founders adapt successfully by building strong executive teams, governance systems, and operational infrastructure. Others struggle with the relentless pressure associated with quarterly expectations, investor scrutiny, media attention, and stock price volatility. Public leadership requires balancing ambition with stability and vision with execution.

Investor psychology also remains one of the most powerful forces shaping capital markets. Markets constantly oscillate between optimism and fear. During speculative periods, investors may prioritize future narratives over present fundamentals. During downturns, they may become excessively focused on risk and short-term survival. Understanding these psychological cycles can help founders and investors navigate markets more intelligently.

The companies that often create the most durable long-term value are those capable of remaining disciplined while others become emotional. They avoid becoming intoxicated by excessive optimism during bull markets and avoid panic during market downturns. Instead, they focus consistently on operational execution, customer value, financial resilience, and strategic adaptability.

Institutional investors play an equally important role within this ecosystem. Capital allocation decisions by hedge funds, pension funds, mutual funds, private equity firms, and asset managers influence which companies scale successfully and which struggle financially. Institutional support can provide credibility, liquidity, operational guidance, and strategic partnerships beyond capital alone.

However, institutional capital is rarely permanent or unconditional. Investors constantly evaluate risk-adjusted return potential based on changing market conditions and operational performance. Companies that maintain transparency, credibility, and execution quality are more likely to sustain long-term investor confidence through difficult cycles.

Regulation and governance also emerged as essential themes throughout this book because public markets function effectively only when trust exists between companies and investors. Transparency, accountability, ethical leadership, accurate financial reporting, and responsible communication form the foundation of healthy capital markets. Weak governance, misleading disclosures, conflicts of interest, or unrealistic projections may temporarily inflate valuations, but they eventually damage credibility and investor confidence.

The rise of SPACs intensified debates regarding how public markets should balance innovation with investor protection. Alternative public offerings expanded access and flexibility, but they also exposed weaknesses in governance and disclosure standards within some transactions. Regulatory evolution will likely continue as markets adapt to technological innovation and changing financial structures.

Looking ahead, the future of public market access may evolve even more dramatically. Artificial intelligence, blockchain systems, tokenized securities, decentralized finance platforms, digital assets, and global investment networks may reshape how companies raise capital and distribute ownership. Traditional financial intermediaries may gradually lose influence as technology enables more direct participation between businesses and investors.

Yet despite these technological changes, the core drivers of long-term wealth creation will likely remain surprisingly consistent.

Companies must still solve meaningful problems.

Customers must still demand products and services.

Leadership must still allocate capital intelligently.

Businesses must still generate sustainable value over time.

Public trust must still be earned and maintained.

Human psychology will likely continue driving cycles of optimism and fear regardless of how advanced financial technology becomes. Investors will continue searching for growth opportunities, entrepreneurs will continue pursuing innovation, and markets will continue rewarding companies capable of adapting successfully to changing environments.

One of the most valuable lessons entrepreneurs can learn from studying alternative public offerings is that access to capital creates leverage. Capital allows businesses to expand faster, hire talent, invest in research, acquire competitors, enter new markets, and scale globally. However, capital itself does not guarantee success. Poor leadership can waste enormous financial resources quickly, while disciplined management may build extraordinary companies even with limited starting resources.

Timing also matters significantly within public markets. Economic conditions, interest rates, liquidity cycles, investor sentiment, and geopolitical events all influence valuations and financing opportunities. Founders and investors who understand market cycles may position themselves more effectively during periods of expansion and contraction.

At the same time, attempting to predict short-term market movements consistently is extremely difficult. Long-term success usually depends less on perfectly timing markets and more on building resilient businesses capable of surviving multiple economic environments over time.

Another major takeaway from this book is the importance of adaptability. Financial markets evolve constantly. Industries transform. Technologies disrupt existing business models. Investor behavior changes. Regulatory frameworks shift. Companies capable of adapting strategically often survive and thrive even as external conditions change dramatically.

The most successful public companies in history were rarely static organizations. They evolved repeatedly across decades while maintaining core strategic strengths. Adaptability, resilience, and long-term thinking often proved more important than temporary market enthusiasm alone.

For investors, understanding alternative public offerings provides valuable insight into how modern wealth creation systems operate. Public markets create opportunities to participate in global innovation and economic growth, but they also involve substantial risks requiring discipline and careful analysis. Long-term investing success usually depends on understanding businesses deeply rather than blindly following speculation or emotional momentum.

For founders, understanding public markets can influence decisions from the earliest stages of entrepreneurship. Ownership structures, capital raising strategy, governance systems, operational discipline, and investor communication all shape long-term outcomes substantially. Small strategic decisions early in a company's development can eventually influence billions of dollars in value creation later.

Ultimately, public offerings are not simply financial transactions. They are transformational events that reshape companies, leadership teams, investor relationships, employee incentives, and long-term strategic possibilities. Alternative public offerings expanded the pathways available for businesses seeking growth and liquidity, but they also reinforced timeless lessons regarding execution, discipline, transparency, and sustainable value creation.

The future will likely bring new public market structures, new financial technologies, and new forms of entrepreneurship that may seem unimaginable today. Some industries discussed throughout this book may transform entirely. Others may disappear while new opportunities emerge. But the foundational principles behind successful public companies will likely endure.

Ownership matters.

Execution matters.

Trust matters.

Discipline matters.

Long-term thinking matters.

Public markets will continue creating enormous opportunities for those capable of understanding these principles and applying them intelligently. Some companies will rise rapidly and disappear just as quickly. Others will survive market cycles, economic crises, technological disruption, and changing investor sentiment to become enduring enterprises shaping industries for generations.

The entrepreneurs and investors who succeed most consistently are often not those chasing temporary excitement, but those capable of building and supporting businesses with real long-term value beneath the market narrative. Public markets may amplify opportunity dramatically, but they also expose weaknesses mercilessly. In the end, sustainable success belongs to those capable of balancing vision with execution, ambition with discipline, and growth with resilience.

Alternative public offerings represented one chapter in the continuing evolution of modern capitalism and financial markets. Many more chapters will follow. The companies, founders, investors, and innovators who understand these systems deeply may position themselves not only to participate in future wealth creation but to help shape the future of the markets themselves.

ambition with discipline, and growth with resilience.

Alternative public offerings represented one chapter in the continuing evolution of modern capitalism and financial markets. Many more chapters will follow. The companies, founders, investors, and innovators who understand these systems deeply may position themselves not only to participate in future wealth creation but to help shape the future of the markets themselves.

www.ingramcontent.com/pod-product-compliance
Lightning Source LLC
LaVergne TN
LVHW040518210926
848480LV00007BA/1503